BIG FOOT KNITS

Big Foot Knits

Library of Congress Control Number: 2013941864
ISBN 13: 978-1-937513-25-2
First Edition
Published by Cooperative Press
www.cooperativepress.com

Patterns and text © 2013, Andi Smith
Photos © 2013, Kristen Caldwell Photography and Cooperative Press
Models: Arabella Proffer, Maria Miranda, Jenny Barnett Rohrs, Andi Smith
Illustrations © 2013, MJ Kim
Background papers © 2013, Terry Cutlip / Sassy Designs
All rights reserved.

Every effort has been made to ensure that all the information in this book is accurate at the time of publication; however, Cooperative Press neither endorses nor guarantees the content of external links referenced in this book.

If you have questions or comments about this book, or need information about licensing, custom editions, special sales, or academic/corporate purchases, please contact Cooperative Press: info@cooperativepress.com or 13000 Athens Ave C288, Lakewood, OH 44107 USA

No part of this book may be reproduced in any form, except brief excerpts for the purpose of review, without prior written permission of the publisher. Thank you for respecting our copyright.

FOR COOPERATIVE PRESS

Senior Editor: Shannon Okey
Assistant Editor: Elizabeth Green Musselman
Technical Editor: Kate Atherley

THIS BOOK IS DEDICATED TO
MY MUM AND MY NAN—
WITHOUT WHOM THE DRIVE
TO UNDERSTAND WOULD BE
SADLY LACKING,

AND TO MARK, COREY,
AND BENJAMIN
WITH THANKS FOR
ABSOLUTELY EVERYTHING.

Contents

Big foot foreword
BY JILLIAN MORENO 7

Author's preface 8

Fitting your foot 9

1: WHAT IS A SOCK? 10
2: MEASURE FOR MEASURE 14
3: GAUGE THE SITUATION 20
4: SHAPING A SHAPELY SOCK 24
5: HOLD IT ALL UP 38
   WITH CUFFS
6: THE WELL-HEELED SOCK 42
7: ROOM FOR TOES 46
8: YOUR OWN 52
   CUSTOM-FIT SOCK
9: BEYOND BASIC 54
   STOCKINETTE

Appendices 125

TECHNIQUES, ... 126
ABBREVIATIONS, & SOCK CARE
ACKNOWLEDGMENTS 129

ABOUT THE AUTHOR 130
ABOUT COOPERATIVE PRESS 131

The patterns 57

PAVARTI 59	MARAMA 65	SELU 73
FREYA 76	EOS 81	ALCYONE 87
ARUNDHATI 93	MIELIKKI 99	SIONNAN 103
EIDOTHEA 107	GAIA 113	ANDRASTE 119

Big foot foreword

As a knitter with a curvy body, I knew when I started knitting that sweater patterns are presented in a sizeist way. They are shown on size S or XS models with little to no curvature to their bodies, and patterns are written with little mention of, or opportunity for, customization.

So I learned how to measure and customize patterns to fit my body. Happily, the knitting world is starting to come out of the dark ages as far as sizing goes, and the discussion and space for altering patterns has opened up considerably.

I used to think that socks were safe, that they were a neutral thing to knit—just a tube. How different could feet be? Then I knit a few pairs of socks. They were too tight in the calf, too long in the foot, too floppy in the heel, and generally ended up in the back of a drawer. I was an unhappy sock knitter.

Then I started taking a closer look at the pictures and the patterns. Sock designers and sock pattern publishers were just as sizeist as the garment folks. Most sock patterns are published in one size (a supposed women's medium) and sized to fit thin calves and long feet. My feet are square and my calves resemble tree trunks. No wonder my socks didn't fit!

I went on to look at the photos in sock patterns—the socks really didn't fit most of the foot models. I saw lots of floppy-looking socks, weird heels, and socks pulled waaay too tightly. Also, most sock patterns have no schematics, and some have no finished measurements at all, which makes customizing for your own feet harder.

In this book, Andi Smith calls bullshit on the average sock pattern. She stands up and tells us why most sock patterns don't fit most feet.

She asks you to do for your feet what you do for the rest of your body: measure and customize so that the socks you knit really fit you. You are a knitter, you have the skills, and Andi gives you the tools.

This book acknowledges the uniqueness of each foot and celebrates it. We knit both to express and comfort ourselves, and having socks that fit exactly honors our skill, our bodies, and our knitterly hearts.

—JILLIAN MORENO
CO-AUTHOR OF *BIG GIRL KNITS*
AND *MORE BIG GIRL KNITS*

Author's preface

LOOKING AT SOCKS IN A WHOLE NEW LIGHT

Why another sock book? After all, there are thousands of sock patterns out there, from the sublime to the divine, from the fancy to the frivolous, so why another one? The answer is pretty simple: as much as we covet and adore the sock patterns, so many of them seem to be designed for those who have narrow feet, ankles, and calves. As one who is not graced with such a shape, I started altering sock patterns until I hit upon an easy, intuitive way to make socks work for any shape or size.

In this book, I'll share those methods and take you step by step through how to measure, calculate, and design everything from a stockinette to an advanced lace sock that fits perfectly and isn't difficult to create. By building on the sock knitting skills you already have, we'll break it all down, build it back up, and end up with socks that fit!

Now, there's no way I can sugarcoat this, but at some point, there's math involved. There's no way to avoid it if you want to alter or create a knitted sock—or any knitted item, for that matter. Never fear, though; we're talking about simple arithmetic: just addition, subtraction, multiplication, division, and percentages. I've created worksheets and tables that guide you through the process to show you not only where you need to apply math, but also why. I've done this to train you to understand the mechanics so that you can apply these same rules and principles to almost any pattern, and to show you that it isn't that hard, complicated, or time-consuming.

All the patterns in the latter half of the book are specifically designed to be easily alterable whilst still looking and feeling amazing.

—ANDI SMITH

FITTING YOUR FOOT

What is a sock?

As we age, wear, and tear, ill-fitting shoes and poor health can change the shape, size, and sensitivity of your feet. However confident you are that you are a size 7 with a 12" ankle, it is worth measuring and reevaluating your feet every few years or so to check on your sizes.

The National Institute on Aging suggests that feet can grow up to a half size every ten years.[1] That can be quite a pinch if you're still squeezing into those size 7s that you wore in your twenties.

Medical problems can also affect how you want your socks to fit. Dry skin, corns, bunions, ingrown toenails, hammer toes, pregnancy, weight gain, and good old swollen feet can radically alter how we want a sock to fit.

Most sock patterns essentially create tubes, with flaps for your heels and flaps for your toes. Worked with the assumption that the leg, ankle, and foot circumferences are the same and worked with a consistent stitch count, this basic tube can be patterned or plain, and is generally designed to fit a foot with an 8–10 inch circumference. Said tube can, and often does, stretch and skim to fit a lot of different shapes and sizes, and when all is said and done, it looks and feels beautiful.

Knitted fabrics can be incredibly forgiving, and, will naturally adjust to fit. If your body does not fall into the standard norm, however, said tube can sometimes leave a lot to be desired. There's nothing worse than spending lots of time, not to mention money, knitting stunning socks that just don't fit, leave an indentation along your calf, fall down constantly, or squash your toes! How many of us have made pair after pair—only to find that they may be OK to wear, they may feel better than store-bought socks (indeed, we can pretty much guarantee that they will)—but they don't quite feel divine. Your feet and calves don't feel like they are swaddled in clouds. If you want a better sock experience, then read on, this is definitely the book for you.

The question needs to be asked: "If a basic sock is a straight tube with shaping for the heels and toes, why not just make a bigger tube?" Surely, socks would be more comfy with a bigger tube?

Well, no. Not really. Then perhaps a simple redesign of the basic tube would be a good idea? What if I give you a design for a sock that has a 17" circumference at the top of the cuff, a 14" ankle and nicely rounded toes? Sure, but only if all us big guys and gals had the same shaped foot and ankle. We don't. No two of us will be shaped exactly the same, and in our considered opinion, that should be celebrated rather than lamented.

Let's take a look at a basic, vanilla sock pattern. It's a great pattern. It's nice and straightforward with all the relevant parts, but as you can see, it's a pattern for a straight-up-and-down tube, with no shaping or modifications.

---

1 http://www.nia.nih.gov/health/publication/foot-care

Vanilla Sock Pattern

Materials

- US #2/2.25mm needles
- 2 skeins of Louet Gems Fingering
- Waste yarn in a similar weight

Gauge: 32 sts = 4"/10cm in St st

TOP-DOWN VERSION

Sock section	8" circumference	10" circumference
Cast on	Using German twisted or other stretchy method, CO 64 sts.	Using German twisted or other stretchy method, CO 80 sts.
Cuff	Being careful not to twist, arrange your sts over your needles and join in the round. Work [k1tbl, p1] rib for 2".	
Leg	Continue working in St st (knit every rnd) for 5".	
Afterthought heel prep	With waste yarn knit 50% of your sts (i.e., 32 sts), then position the sts to knit again. Re-knit the sts with your sock yarn and continue knitting.	With waste yarn knit 50% of your sts (i.e., 40 sts), then position the sts to knit again. Re-knit the sts with your sock yarn and continue knitting.
Foot	Continue working in St st (knit every rnd) for 8".	
Toe	Rnd 1: [K1, ssk, k26, k2tog, k1] twice. Rnd 2: Knit. Rnd 3: [K1, ssk, k24, k2tog, k1] twice. Rnd 4: Knit.	Rnd 1: [K1, ssk, k34, k2tog, k1] twice. Rnd 2: Knit. Rnd 3: [K1, ssk, k32, k2tog, k1] twice. Rnd 4: Knit.
	Continue working decs as established every other rnd until 32 sts rem. Use kitchener stitch or 3-needle bind off to graft rem sts.	Continue working decs as established every other rnd until 40 sts rem. Use kitchener stitch or 3-needle bind off to graft rem sts.
Afterthought heel	Using one needle for the leg sts and one needle for the foot sts, pick up the sts from the waste yarn. Knit 1 rnd, then work the heel as you did the toe.	
Finishing	Weave in ends and block.	

TOE-UP VERSION

Sock section	8" circumference	10" circumference
Cast on	Using Judy's Magic Cast On method, CO 32 sts. Divide your sts on your needles.	Using Judy's Magic Cast On method, CO 40 sts. Divide your sts on your needles.
Toe	Rnd 1: Knit. Rnd 2: [K1, m1, k14, m1, k1] twice. Rnd 3: Knit. Rnd 4: [K1, m1, k16, m1, k1] twice. Continue alternating a plain St st rnd with an increase rnd, placing the increases in the same places, until you have 64 sts.	Rnd 1: Knit. Rnd 2: [K1, m1, k18, m1, k1] twice. Rnd 3: Knit. Rnd 4: [K1, m1, k20, m1, k1] twice. Continue alternating a plain St st rnd with an increase rnd, placing the increases in the same places, until you have 80 sts.
Foot	Continue working in St st (knit every rnd) for 8".	
Afterthought heel prep	With waste yarn, knit 50% of the sts, then slip sts back to left-hand needle. Re-knit the same sts with your sock yarn.	
Leg	Continue working in St st for 5".	
Cuff	Work [k1tbl, p1] rib for 2" and bind off.	
Afterthought heel	Slip the sts that are currently on the waste yarn back onto needles, using one needle for the leg sts and one needle for the foot sts. Knit 1 rnd, then work decs as follows:	
	Rnd 1: [K1, ssk, k26, k2tog, k1] twice. Rnd 2: Knit. Rnd 3: [K1, ssk, k24, k2tog, k1] twice. Rnd 4: Knit. Continue working decs as established ever alternate rnd until 32 sts rem. Use kitchener or 3-needle bind off to graft the rem sts.	Rnd 1: [K1, ssk, k34, k2tog, k1] twice. Rnd 2: Knit. Rnd 3: [K1, ssk, k32, k2tog, k1] twice. Rnd 4: Knit. Continue working decs as established ever alternate rnd until 40 sts rem. Use kitchener or 3-needle bind off to graft the rem sts.
Finishing	Weave in ends and block.	

This is a good basic sock pattern; however, it is still an unshaped tube. Negative ease can make that sock fit a leg and foot that is 10–15% larger, but because of the inherent variations in the circumference of the foot and leg, this sock isn't going to fit particularly well. Some sections will be stretched more than others, and an over-stretched fabric is not only less comfortable to wear, it's also less durable and less visually pleasing.

As you do your initial flip through this book, you'll notice that there are about a million worksheets and charts. Please don't be daunted. When all is said and done, it will take you about an hour to do all the measuring and math to create your custom sock. I break down and explain each step in the following chapters, and then bring it all together into one master sock worksheet, and then move on to explaining how to modify existing patterns. Finally, I share a few patterns of my own, written specifically with alteration in mind.

A NOTE ON MY SOCK CONSTRUCTION

In this book, I make a few departures from more conventional sock knitting and construction. The first thing you may notice as you read through is that I don't have gussets in my socks. This is because I've found that if you alter the circumference of your socks frequently to reflect the changes in your shape, this eliminates the need for gussets. In other words, the lovely form-fitting shaping that gussets offer is still built into my socks, but I've distributed that shaping across the whole sock.

I also focus on afterthought heels, rather than heel flaps, short-row heels, or the myriad other possibilities that are out there. There are a few reasons for this decision. Firstly, I like afterthought heels. And really, isn't knitting all about choosing what we like? Secondly, they work best for my method of increasing and decreasing throughout a sock. Thirdly, I like the flow of working a stitch pattern without breaking for a heel, and finally, from personal preference, I like the adaptability of the shape.

My preferred method of knitting socks is to provisionally cast on for the toe section; I then knit up to the cuff of the sock, and finally work an afterthought heel and a top-down toe. Born out of the desire to use every scrap of yarn, but being unsure of the length that I could achieve in the leg, this method works well for me. I don't enjoy knitting short-row heels and toes, so this method just evolved and now I love it.

Please don't feel limited by the choices I've made. Apply your own favorite methodology. Really, it's all about making the actual knitting experience enjoyable as well as productive!

WHAT'S IN STORE

In the following chapters, I'll show you how to design a sock tube specifically for you.

I'll show you how to knit beautiful socks that fit, feel, and look wonderful no matter how your tootsies are built.

I'll show you how to evaluate your unique foot shape and how to choose patterns that work for you.

I'll show you how to work shaping into patterns you may already have.

In short, I'll show you just what you need not only to knit socks, but to knit socks that are stunning to look at and comfortable to wear, that are shaped for *you*.

Measure for measure

With 26 bones, 107 ligaments, 33 joints, and 19 muscles and tendons, the foot is indeed a complex creature. No wonder our feet vary so much in shape and size.

The Craft Yarn Council's measurement standards[1] suggest that the average woman's foot circumference is between 7 and 9 inches and that average foot length is between 9 and 11 inches. I'd like to respectfully challenge that standard. We are not average beings, and our feet are not average sizes.

Therefore, it stands to reason that individually sized sock patterns are the way to go. But it is impractical for designers to create socks that offer individual fit for each and every person. We need to learn to do this part for ourselves.

By determining our specific measurements, it is possible to break down a basic sock pattern and add or remove stitches and rounds to make a more comfortable, well-fitting sock.

So let's start with those measurements. By having an accurate picture of these, we can map out just how your unique sock will look.

CREATE YOUR OWN PERSONAL MEASUREMENTS CHART

Have a measuring party! Similar to measuring parties for sweaters, a second person doing the measuring always helps get accurate figures. And reciprocate—it's twice the fun!

You will need a pencil, a cloth tape measure, and the chart on the following page.

---

1 http://www.craftyarncouncil.com/footsize.html

Try to measure your feet in the evening, or after you've been standing for a while. Get them when they're at their grandest!

- Stand with your feet a shoulder's width apart. Relax your calf muscles.
- Follow the measuring guide to mark down all your vitals for each foot.

In two places in your measuring chart, you will be asked for your average foot and leg circumferences. To find an average number:

- Add all the numbers together.
- Divide that number by the number of numbers you added together.

For example: if the circumference of your foot at five different points measures 7, 7, 8, 9 and 12 and we want to find the average foot circumference, then adding these numbers together gives us 43. Since we added five numbers together, we divide 43 by 5 to get 8.6, which is the average of our original five numbers.

DON'T CHEAT (AND WHY)

It's easy to be unhappy with your measurements; it's basic human nature to be dissatisfied with how you look. However, if you keep to your true measurements, you will create a well-fitting sock that skims your curves rather than pinches them, and looks and feels much better than an ill-fitting one.

As you look at your measurements, you may be surprised by how many variables there are.

MEASURING FEET

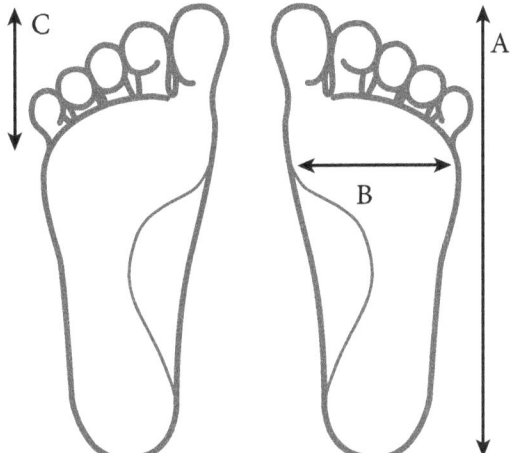
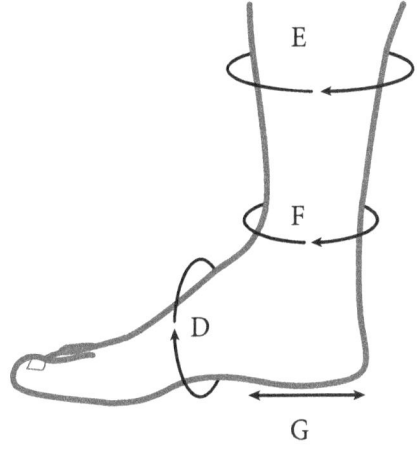

A – foot length

B – foot circumference at toe join

    B1 – foot circumference at 1" below B

    B2 – foot circumference at 2" below B

    B3 – foot circumference at 3" below B

    B4 – foot circumference at 4" below B

    B5 – foot circumference at 5" below B

    B6 – foot circumference at 6" below B

    B7 – foot circumference at 7" below B

    B8 – foot circumference at 8" below B

C – toe height (length from curve of little toe to top of big toe)

D – foot circumference at ankle

E – leg circumference at base of knee

F – leg circumference at ankle

    F1 – leg circumference 1" above ankle

    F2 – leg circumference 2" above ankle

    F3 – leg circumference 3" above ankle

    F4 – leg circumference 4" above ankle

    F5 – leg circumference 5" above ankle

    F6 – leg circumference 6" above ankle

    F7 – leg circumference 7" above ankle

    F8 – leg circumference 8" above ankle

    F9 – leg circumference 9" above ankle

    F10 – leg circumference 10" above ankle

    F11 – leg circumference 11" above ankle

    F12 – leg circumference 12" above ankle

    F13 – leg circumference 13" above ankle

    F14 – leg circumference 14" above ankle

    F15 – leg circumference 15" above ankle

    F16 – leg circumference 16" above ankle

G – heel depth (length from base of D to back of foot)

Why these numbers matter: an example

If we look at the measurements for three knitters, we can see that their numbers are all different. Notice, for instance, that while Celeste and Betty have the same foot length (measurement A), and probably wear the same size shoe, their foot circumference (measurement B) is quite different.

Where to measure	Sally	Celeste	Betty
Foot measurements			
A – foot length	9"	10.5"	10.5"
B – foot circumference at toe join	9"	13"	10"
B1 – foot circumference at 1" below B	8"	13"	9.5"
B2 – foot circumference at 2" below B	8"	12"	9"
B3 – foot circumference at 3" below B	8.5"	12"	9.5"
B4 – foot circumference at 4" below B	9"	11.5"	9.5"
B5 – foot circumference at 5" below B	9"	11.5"	10"
B6 – foot circumference at 6" below B	n/a	11"	10"
B7 – foot circumference at 7" below B	n/a	11"	n/a
B8 – foot circumference at 8" below B	n/a	n/a	n/a
Average foot circumference	*8.64"*	*11.77"*	*9.75"*
C – toe height	1.5"	2.75"	2.5"
D – foot circumference at ankle	9"	11"	10"
G – heel depth	3"	2.5"	3"
Leg measurements			
E – leg circumference at base of knee	16"	21"	16"
F – leg circumference at ankle	9.5"	14"	12"
F1 – leg circumference 1" above ankle	10"	15.5"	13.5"
F2 – leg circumference 2" above ankle	11"	15.5"	13.5"
F3 – leg circumference 3" above ankle	11.5"	16"	14"
F4 – leg circumference 4" above ankle	12"	16"	14"
F5 – leg circumference 5" above ankle	14"	17"	14"
F6 – leg circumference 6" above ankle	14"	17"	14.5"
F7 – leg circumference 7" above ankle	15"	17"	15"
F8 – leg circumference 8" above ankle	15"	18"	15"
F9 – leg circumference 9" above ankle	16"	19"	15"
F10 – leg circumference 10" above ankle	16"	20"	15"
F11 – leg circumference 11" above ankle	n/a	20.5"	16"
F12 – leg circumference 12" above ankle	n/a	n/a	16"
F13 – leg circumference 13" above ankle	n/a	n/a	16.5"
F14 – leg circumference 14" above ankle	n/a	n/a	n/a
F15 – leg circumference 15" above ankle	n/a	n/a	n/a
F16 – leg circumference 16" above ankle	n/a	n/a	n/a
Average leg circumference	*13.33"*	*17.42"*	*14.66"*

Taking your own measurements

Now let's move on to analyzing the shapes of our own legs and feet.

What you will need:

- a measuring partner
- 2 pieces of paper each
- a pencil

Part of foot	What to do	Your left foot/leg results (circle one)	Your right foot/leg results (circle one)
Overall foot shape	Have your measuring partner draw around both of your feet. One foot just won't do. You'd be surprised just how many people's feet are not only differently sized but also differently shaped from each other.	Standard, wider at the toe, square, or wider at the heel?	Standard, wider at the toe, square, or wider at the heel?
Toe shape	Look at the outline of your toes. Which of the drawings at right best describes your toes on each foot?	Round, tapered, square, or left-sloped?	Round, tapered, square, or right-sloped?
Heel shape	To analyze your heels, have your measuring partner look at your heels from the back. Note how your heels sit in relation to the floor, and look at them in relation to your ankles.	Round, square, or pointed?	Round, square, or pointed?
Leg shape	Regardless of the girth of your legs, the actual shape of them is going to fall into one of the basic categories at right.		

ANALYZING YOUR MEASUREMENTS

Now that we have all your parts measured, analyzed and documented, it's time to think about what it all means.

If we look at the measurements for our basic sock tube, both the foot and leg measures either 8 or 10" in circumference.

If we look at our three stalwart examples, their average foot and leg circumferences are as follows:

	Sally	Celeste	Betty
Average foot circumference	8.64"	11.77"	9.75"
Average leg circumference	13.33"	17.42"	14.66"

Sally's and Betty's foot circumferences would fit comfortably into a typical sock, while Celeste's feet would be too long—and all three women's legs are too wide for the basic sock.

In each instance, we can see that their foot and leg circumferences are not identical, so working a standard sock tube in a larger size would not create a well-fitted sock for any of them.

We will be visiting the examples above throughout the book and use these knitters' numbers to illustrate how to do the math and adapt patterns.

As we move through the book from this point on we'll also use the numbers that you've gathered in this section to create your own custom pattern. As you proceed through the chapters, look out for your own mix of icons to show you not only which techniques and shapes work for you, but also how to create custom ones specifically for your fit.

My personal measurements chart

FOOT MEASUREMENTS	left foot	right foot
A – foot length		
B – foot circumference at toe join		
B1 – foot circumference at 1" below B		
B2 – foot circumference at 2" below B		
B3 – foot circumference at 3" below B		
B4 – foot circumference at 4" below B		
B5 – foot circumference at 5" below B		
B6 – foot circumference at 6" below B		
B7 – foot circumference at 7" below B		
B8 – foot circumference at 8" below B		
Average foot circumference		
C – toe height		
D – foot circumference at ankle		
G – heel depth		
LEG MEASUREMENTS	**left leg**	**right leg**
E – leg circumference at base of knee		
F – leg circumference at ankle		
F1 – leg circumference 1" above ankle		
F2 – leg circumference 2" above ankle		
F3 – leg circumference 3" above ankle		
F4 – leg circumference 4" above ankle		
F5 – leg circumference 5" above ankle		
F6 – leg circumference 6" above ankle		
F7 – leg circumference 7" above ankle		
F8 – leg circumference 8" above ankle		
F9 – leg circumference 9" above ankle		
F10 – leg circumference 10" above ankle		
F11 – leg circumference 11" above ankle		
F12 – leg circumference 12" above ankle		
F13 – leg circumference 13" above ankle		
F14 – leg circumference 14" above ankle		
F15 – leg circumference 15" above ankle		
F16 – leg circumference 16" above ankle		
Average leg circumference		

Gauge the situation

I have a love/hate relationship with gauge, as I think many of us do. The thought of having to delay your new knitting project to knit a swatch—not to mention wash, dry, measure, and sometimes re-knit that swatch on different needles—seems to be the worst kind of torture for those of us who are eager to get going on a project!

However, I've learned through trial and (much) error, that gauge really is important. We've all made the mistake of eagerly knitting something with the absolute certainty that our gauge matches the gauge given in the pattern without having to check it, only to find that your finished garment would best fit a creature from Picasso's abstract period—devastating!

It's true that when faced with a gauge swatch for a sock, you may look at the number of stitches and rounds and decide you may as well just go ahead and knit the sock, but if you want a sock that fits, it's really worth the time and effort to swatch and block. Look at it this way: you've gone to all the trouble of buying and reading this book, spent money on great yarn, taken measurements, and are eager to move forward with well-fitting socks, why not go that extra step? Look upon gauge as insurance!

Gauge is also essential when it comes to increases and decreases. You may know that you need to decrease the circumference by 1½ inches at point x, but without an accurate count of how many stitches and rounds you knit per inch, you'll be guesstimating at best.

Your gauge is going to be different for ribbing than it is for stockinette or many stitch patterns, hence the need for two different swatches. Basically, if your sock pattern has a different pattern for the cuff than for the body, then make two separate swatches. By working two different swatches, we eliminate the transition between patterns which can warp the shape and size of stitches within the transition, which would throw off an accurate gauge count.

While working your swatches, take time to find the perfect cast on and bind off for your sock. On each of your swatches, try the different cast on and bind off techniques section discussed at the end of the book (page 126). Once you have blocked your swatch, stretch it as much as you can and see how it bounces back. Does it affect the rounds below? Does it have good bounce back? This is the ideal opportunity to find the techniques that work perfectly for your socks.

A LITTLE NEGATIVITY GOES A LONG WAY

Negativity in ease, that is! Ease refers to the way in which a garment fits you. Things with positive ease are loose, not form-fitting. Things with negative ease are actually slightly smaller than your body measurements, creating a tighter fit. Negative ease is especially important in socks as it allows the stitches to grip your skin, keeping those socks up and contouring to your shape. Loose socks have a habit of forming fabric flaps inside your shoes and falling down your legs, which is most uncomfortable.

In order to create a well-fitting sock, we need a sock that has just the right amount of negative ease, so that it's not too loose or tight, but has exactly the right number of stitches to hug those curves comfortably. A good rule of thumb is to subtract 10% from your actual measurements for a snugly fitting sock or 5% for slightly more ease.

HOW TO WORK THE PERFECT GAUGE SWATCH FOR SOCKS

Needles and yarn
Work with the same needles and yarn that you'll be using for the sock. We're aiming for a sample that's as true a representation of your final sock as possible, so keep things the same.

The "pattern"
Cast on about 40 stitches using your favorite stretchy method. I prefer to use the German Twisted cast on (see page 126), but there are so many good ones out there—find one that works for you!

Be sure to work your swatch in the round. Working in the round produces a different gauge than working flat does. Purl stitches are actually slightly taller than knit stitches, and so rounds knitted in stockinette (knit every round) will vary from rows (knit one row, purl one row).

Work about 2" of your rib choice. Any less and you won't get a true picture of the number of rounds per inch. Bind off.

Using the same cast-on method, cast on about 40 stitches (or the closest multiple of your stitch pattern) and work about 2" of your body pattern and bind off. Initially, we'll just be using stockinette; however, in later chapters, we'll be introducing lace, twisted stitches, and cables. The same principles apply regardless of the pattern; however, the stitch count may have to change depending on your pattern.

At least 2" of both the rib and body pattern are needed to accurately find both your round and stitch gauge.

Wet block both swatches (see page 128) and dry thoroughly.

HOW TO MEASURE YOUR SWATCHES

The body
To find the number of stitches per inch:

1. Lay your swatch on a flat surface or board, without stretching it.

2. Measure the swatch by laying a flat ruler along a line of stitches.

3. Count the number of stitches in 2", then divide that number by 2 to determine stitches per inch.

4. Decrease that number by 5–10% (that is, multiply your stitches/inch number by 0.05 or 0.1) to allow for negative ease.

5. Fold the work so that the "edges" are in the center and re-measure. Sometimes, those first couple of stitches can have a different gauge to the rest of your work. If you find this to be the case, one method I like to teach is to knit the first stitch, put the right-hand needle in the second stitch, wrap the yarn as if to knit and then give it a tug. This tightens up the first stitch without over-tightening it and making it smaller than its neighbors.

To find the number of rounds per inch:

1. Lay your swatch on a flat surface or board, without stretching it.
2. Measure the swatch by laying a flat ruler along a column of stitches.

3. Count the number of stitches in 2", then divide that number by 2 to determine rounds per inch.
4. Decrease by 5% or 10% to allow for negative ease.
5. Fold the work so that the "edges" are actually in the center and re-measure.

Remember, rounds-per-inch is the vertical measurement and stitches-per-inch is the horizontal.

NEGATIVE EASE CHEAT SHEETS

# sts per rnd	10%	new # sts per rnd (i.e., sts minus 10%)
6	0.6	5.4
7	0.7	6.3
8	0.8	7.2
9	0.9	8.1
10	1.0	9
11	1.1	9.9
12	1.2	10.8
13	1.3	11.7
14	1.4	12.6

# sts per rnd	5%	new # sts per rnd (i.e., sts minus 5%)
6	0.3	5.7
7	0.3.5	6.65
8	0.4	7.6
9	0.4.5	8.55
10	0.5	9.5
11	0.55	10.45
12	0.6	11.4
13	0.65	12.35
14	0.7	13.3

Use this table to record your results:

MY STOCKINETTE GAUGE	
yarn	
needles	
sts per inch	
negative ease %	
gauge (sts per inch − negative ease)	

The cuff

Measuring gauge on the cuff portion of a swatch is a two-step process. You first measure as you did above in steps 1–3 (not 4) for the body of the sock. You then re-measure the cuff after stretching it as much as possible, following steps 1–4.

Next, we add both these numbers together and divide them by 2. Because cuffs are by nature a more elastic fabric than stockinette, this method of finding a good percentage of negative ease is most practical.

Repeat step 5.

If you end up with a fraction of a number, that's OK—once you've determined how many total stitches you'll be starting with, round down to make a whole number.

Those fraction-of-a-stitch measurements are important until you have a stitch count for your whole project.

For example, if your gauge was 12.7 stitches per inch and you had a circumference of 14 inches, then your project stitch count would be 177.8 (which you can then round up or down to a convenient whole number).

However, if you had rounded down to 12 sts per inch, then your stitch count would be 168—a difference of almost 10 sts and almost an inch of stitches lost.

Use the following table to record your results:

MY RIB GAUGE	
yarn	
needles	
pattern	
sts per inch	
negative ease %	
gauge (sts per inch − negative ease)	

Now you have accurate measurements and gauge, along with a clear picture of all the different parts of your leg and foot that are involved in knitting a well-fitting, comfortable sock. If you've found that you have similar average circumferences in both your leg and foot and that you have standard icons for your toes, heels, instep and foot shape, feel free to jump ahead to chapter 8 (page 52), where I'll show you how to build your perfect sock.

If you have lots of different shapes going on, then continue reading as we look at ways we can change the basic sock tube to better fit our unique feet.

Shaping a shapely sock

Before we begin to manipulate our basic sock tube, we need to take a closer look at the engines that drive that change—namely increases and decreases. Let's look not only at the different types, but also at when it's appropriate to use them, what job they do, and how to work out the math for maintaining our new comfortable sock shape.

TYPES OF DECREASES

We have three types of decrease available to us—the left-leaning, the right-leaning, and the central double decrease. If decreases are going to occur randomly and will be spaced far apart, then any decrease can be used. However, if you are working a column of decreases, then consider which type of decrease will best suit the overall pattern.

Left-leaning decreases

Traditionally used at the beginning of a round or to the left of center within a round, these decreases orient the stitches to the left. There are two main left-leaning decreases we use, the ssk and the skp.

- **ssk**—Slip the first stitch as if to knit, slip the second stitch as if to purl then knit them both together through the back of the loop. Many people slip both stitches as if to knit, but if you slip the second stitch as if to purl, the line created is smoother and more comparable to the k2tog.

- **skp**—Slip 1, k1, psso. Slip the first stitch as if to purl, knit the second stitch, pass the first stitch over the second.

I find the skp less visually pleasing than the ssk. I also find that it breaks the flow of knitting more than an ssk or k2tog, because of the more pronounced use of the left-hand needle to pass the slipped stitch over. Quite honestly, though, either one of these left-leaning decreases is fine to use.

Right-leaning decrease

Typically used at the end or to the right of the center of a round, these decreases orient the stitches to the right and create a smooth line within your work. The method we use is k2tog.

Shaping a shapely sock

- **k2tog**—Knit 2 stitches together. A nice, smooth, right-leaning line is created by this decrease. Nice and simple.

Central double decreases
Traditionally used in the center of a round or the center of a group of stitches.

- **sk2po**— Slip 1 st knitwise, k2tog, and pass the slipped st over. This decrease reduces 3 stitches down to one. It pulls in one stitch from either side, and although it doesn't create a lean in the fabric, the stitch lying on top of the decrease does lean to the left.

- **s2kpo**—Slip 2 sts tog as if to k2tog, k1, pass the 2 slipped sts over. This decrease also takes 3 sts and reduces them to one. It's centered, in that it doesn't have a particular lean—it pulls in a stitch from either side toward the central stitch. The visual created is balanced and pleasing: a strong vertical line with a stitch leaning in on either side.

TYPES OF INCREASES

- **yarnovers (yo)**—To make a yo in stockinette, bring the yarn to the front as if about to purl, then knit the next stitch. The yarn will fall over the right-hand needle and land behind the stitch knitted.

As you can see, yarnovers create holes, which can be a pretty design detail. This can be great if used within a cuff or within a lace pattern.

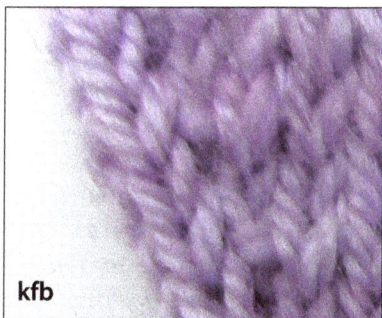

- **knit front and back (kfb)**—Knit the next stitch as usual, but leave the original stitch on the left-hand needle, then knit through the back loop of it.

As you can see in the photo above, kfb increases are virtually invisible. These work well within swaths of stockinette.

- **make 1 left (m1L)**—Find the bar between the stitch just worked and the next stitch on the LH needle; insert LH needle under this bar from front to back, then knit through the back loop. This creates a left-leaning increase and orients your stitches to the left.

- **make 1 right (m1R)**—Find the bar between the stitch just worked and the next one on the LH needle; insert LH needle under this bar from back to front, then knit through the front loop. This creates a right-leaning increase and your stitches will lean to the right.

- **double increase (m2)**—M1L, then k1 and m1R. This method is the increase twin of the central double decrease. The central stitch will look unchanged, whilst the stitches on either side will look as if they are disappearing into it.

I prefer to use the m1 methods when knitting socks, especially for stockinette, but which you should choose really comes down to personal preference.

Deciding where and how to decrease or increase will depend on three main factors:

- how many rounds you want to decrease or increase over
- how many points within each round you want to decrease or increase
- what type of decrease or increase you will use

To determine how many stitches you need to decrease, subtract your end number from your start number then decide over how many rounds you want your decreases to happen.

In the table below, I've listed three examples, each with different scenarios for decreases. Below that, I've taken these examples and shown you how to work out what to do where.

	start #	end #	# to dec	# of rnds
Example 1a	104	86	18	1
Example 1b	104	86	18	2
Example 1c	104	86	18	18
Example 1d	104	86	18	9
Example 2a	112	90	22	1
Example 2b	112	90	22	2
Example 2c	112	90	22	22
Example 2d	112	90	22	11
Example 3a	108	74	34	1
Example 3b	108	74	34	2
Example 3c	108	74	34	34
Example 3d	108	74	34	17

Now that we know by how many stitches we're going to change our base number, we can decide how those changes are going to happen.

I like to classify my decreases into two categories, the Short and the Long Decrease.

THE SHORT DECREASE

A short decrease occurs over one or two rounds and at many points within the stitch count. This decrease is best utilized at the point between cuff and body or at any time when you want an even decrease throughout the width of your work.

How to work a short decrease
First, we need to determine how many stitches there are between each decrease in order to create an even look.

If you have a nice simple number like 100 stitches which you want to decrease down to 90 stitches, take your initial number and divide by the number you want to decrease by.

In this case, 100 ÷ 10 = 10, so you know you have ten groups of 10 in which to work a decrease, ergo, you would work [k8, decrease] 10 times. Simple.

start #	end #	# to dec	# of rnds	patt
100	90	10	1	[K8, dec] 10 times

You can't guarantee that you will always get a number that is so easily divisible, however, so a little playing with numbers needs to happen.

Applying a short decrease to the previous three examples would look something like this:

Example 1a

start #	end #	# to dec	# of rnds
104	86	18	1

1. start #	104
2. end #	86
3. # to dec	18
4. # of rnds to dec	1
5. step 1 divided by step 3	104 / 18 = 5.77 *If the result of step 5 is not a whole number then find the nearest lower number that is divisible by step 3.*
6. nearest # divisible by #3	5 × 18 = 90
7. base #	The number we multiply #3 by to get our nearest lower number. *5 × 18 = 90 our base # is 5*
8. # of sts remaining	104 − 90 = 14
9. # of groups with an extra stitch	14 groups with 5 sts plus 1 st = 6 *14 groups of 6 sts*
10. # of groups with base number of sts	18 − 14 = 4 *4 groups of 5 sts*
11. pattern	[K4, dec] 14 times, [k3, dec] 4 times = 86 sts

Here's how this worked: Steps 1–4 of the table are the numbers we have to work with.

In Step 5 we divide the original stitch count by step 3—in this instance, 104 ÷ 18 = 5.77

Step 6: Since this isn't a whole number, we have to find the nearest whole number that is divisible by step 3. We know that we are working with 18 groups of stitches and each of the groups will have at least 5 stitches (the number by which we multiplied to reach our nearest whole number).

Step 7: This is our base number, which is the lowest number of stitches we will have in each of our groups of stitches to decrease.

Step 8: Work out the difference between step 1 and step 6 (104 − 90 = 14).

Step 9: The number of groups of stitches that will have 1 extra stitch—in this instance, there are 14 extra stitches that are spread 1 stitch over 14 groups of stitches.

Step 10: This is the number of groups of stitches that do not have an extra an extra stitch.

Step 11: The resulting pattern.

	start #	end #	# to dec	# of rnds
Example 2a	112	90	22	1

1.	start #	112
2.	end #	90
3.	# to dec	22
4.	# of rnds to dec	1
5.	step 1 divided by step 3	112 ÷ 22 = 5.09
		If the result of step 5 is not a whole number, then find the nearest lower number that is divisible by step 3.
6.	nearest # divisible by #3	5 × 22 = 110
7.	base #	The number we multiply step 3 by to get our nearest lower number
		5 × 22 = 110 our base # is 5
8.	# of sts remaining	112 − 110 = 2
9.	# of groups with an extra stitch	2 groups with 5 sts plus 1st = 6
		2 groups of 6 sts
10.	# of groups with base number of sts	22 − 2 = 20
		20 groups of 5 sts
11.	pattern	[K3, decrease] 20 times, [k4, decrease] twice = 90 sts

Shaping a shapely sock

	start #	end #	# to dec	# of rnds
Example 3a	108	74	34	1

1.	start #	108
2.	end #	74
3.	# to dec	34
4.	# of rnds to dec	1
5.	step 1 divided by step 3	108 ÷ 34 = 3.17 *If the result of step 5 is not a whole number, find the nearest lower number that is divisible by #3.*
6.	nearest # divisible by #3	3 × 34 = 102
7.	base #	The number we multiply #3 by to get our nearest lower number. *3 × 34 = 102 our base # is 3*
8.	# of sts remaining	108 − 102 = 6
9.	# of groups with an extra stitch	6 groups with base # plus 1 *6 groups of 3 plus 1 = 4 sts*
10.	# of groups with base number of sts	34 − 6 = 28 *28 groups of 3 sts*
11.	pattern	[K1, decrease] 28 times, [k2, decrease] 6 times = 74 sts

Use the following worksheet to calculate the short decreases for your own socks:

MY SHORT DECREASE WORKSHEET	
1. start #	
2. end #	
3. # to dec	
4. # of rnds to dec	
5. step 1 divided by step 3	
6. nearest # divisible by #3	
7. base #	
8. # of sts remaining	
9. # of groups with an extra stitch	
10. # of groups with base number of sts	
11. pattern	

One of the things that I appreciate most about knitting is that there is no absolute right way of doing things. Even within the basic short decrease as explained above, there are lots of ways that you can change it up. You could have all the larger groups of stitches grouped together, or you may space the larger stitch groups evenly amongst the shorter stitch groups, or any combination of the above. It's all a matter of personal preference.

If decreasing all the stitches needed in one round is not what you prefer, you may choose to work two short decrease rounds. I like to leave at least one round between decreases to make the lines more seamless, but again, it's entirely up to you. The math is very similar to the short decreases described above.

	start #	end #	# to dec	# of rnds
Example 1b	104	86	18	2

1.	start #	104
2.	end #	86
3.	# to dec	18
4.	# of rnds to dec	2
5.	# of sts to dec each rnd	Step 3 divided by Step 2 18 ÷ 2 = 9
6.	step 1 divided by step 5	104 ÷ 9 = 11.55 *If the result of step 6 is not a whole number, then find the nearest lower number that is divisible by step 5.*
7.	nearest # divisible by step 3	11 × 9 = 99
8.	base #	The number we multiply step 6 by to get our nearest lower number. 11
9.	# of sts remaining	104 − 99 = 5
10.	# of groups with an extra stitch	5 groups with base # plus 1 or 5 groups with 11 + 1 = 12
11.	# of groups with base number of sts	4 groups with base or 4 groups with 11
12.	first rnd of pattern	Rnd 1: [K10, single decrease] 5 times, [k9, single decrease] 4 times = 95 sts. Rnd 2: Knit. Rnd 3: [K9, single decrease] 5 times, [k8, single decrease] 4 times = 86 sts.

Just as in example 1a, we know we have to decrease by 18 stitches; however, this time, we will do the math to do this over 2 rounds.

18 divided by 2 is 9, so we will decrease each round by 9 sts.

After the first round we will be left with 95 stitches and after the second decrease round, we'll be left with 86 stitches.

This time we will divide the starting number by 9, work out the formula for that pattern round, then take the next round number of stitches (95) and divide that by 9 to work out that round of decreases.

104 − 9 sts = 95 sts

104 ÷ 9 = 11.55

The nearest number to 104 divisible by 9 is 99 with a remainder of 5.

We will need a total of 9 groups of stitches to divide into, so we will use 5 groups of stitches with the divisor (11) plus 1 and 4 groups of stitches that are the same as the divisor, or, to put it another way, 5 groups of 12 and 4 groups of 11.

The pattern row would look as follows:

Rnd 1: [K10, dec] 5 times, [k9, dec] 4 times—95 sts.
Rnd 2 (or more rnds): Knit.
Next Rnd: [K9, dec] 5 times, [k8, dec] 4 times—86 sts.

The same system would apply to examples 2b and 3b.

THE LONG DECREASE

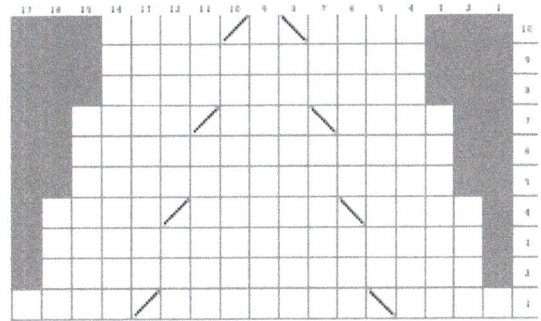

A long decrease occurs over more than two rounds and happens at the same point within the stitch count each time. It's best utilized when you want to add a subtle decrease in one area of the sock, such as the center back of the leg or on the instep.

How to work a long decrease
First, take the number of stitches you want to decrease and divide that by the number of rounds you want to decrease over.

	start #	end #	# of sts to dec	# of rnds
Example 1c	108	86	18	18

As we look a this example, we see that we will be decreasing 18 stitches over 18 rounds.

I would not recommend using a single decrease at the same point in this instance because aesthetically, it would not look good and would make your sock lopsided.

You could, however, work a double decrease in the same place 9 times or paired decreases at two spots every second round.

Let's assume you want to work a double decrease along the center back of your sock. Let's also assume that you are working on two needles, the front of your sock being on the first needle and the back of the sock on the second—54 stitches on each needle. This is another one of those instances where number fudging comes into play. Since we want the line of decreases to run down the center, but have an even number of stitches, the decrease will actually fall one stitch off-center. Visually, only the most eagle-eyed of knitters will be able to tell, and then only if you tell them!

Example 1c
Rnd 1: Knit first needle, k25, work double dec, knit to end.
Rnd 2: Knit.
Rnd 3: Knit first needle, k24, work double dec, knit to end.
Rnd 4: Knit.
… and so on.

If you choose to decrease at two points, you may wish to use a paired decrease in that you will have a left-leaning and a right-leaning decrease, which will visually keep your work balanced.

You may choose to decrease at the beginning of each alternate round, or at set points within the round. Check out the examples of decreases at the end of this chapter to help you choose the one you prefer.

As you can imagine, there are lots of variables and possibilities when it comes to decreasing within your sock. But you can make the process easier with just a little addition and subtraction.

Increasing within your sock
As with decreases, I like to classify the increases into two categories—short increases, which happen over 1 or 2 rounds, and long increases, which happen over more than 2 rounds. The math used is basically a reversal of the math we used when working our decreases.

THE SHORT INCREASE

Worked over 1 round or 3 rounds, with a round of plain knitting in between, short increases are great for adding width in the leg of the sock where circumference changes can happen quickly.

If we are working with numbers that are easily divisible, then the math would look like this:

start #	end #	# of sts to dec	# of rnds
90	100	10	1

Then the working out would look like this:

Step 1: start #	90
Step 2: end #	100
Step 3: # of sts to inc	10
Step 4: # of rnds	1

Shaping a shapely sock

Step 5: find base # of each group to increase	Step 1 divided by Step 3
	90 ÷ 10 = 9; base # is 9
Step 6: pattern	Base # increased by 1
	Rnd 1: [K8, m1] 10 times.

MY SHORT INCREASE WORKSHEET (SIMPLE VERSION)	
Step 1: start #	
Step 2: end #	
Step 3: # of sts to inc	
Step 4: # of rnds	
Step 5: find base # of each group to increase	
Step 6: pattern	

However, just like in decreasing, we cannot always count on our math resulting in whole numbers. When that is the case, work the math like this (using the numbers in example 1a):

	start #	end #	# of sts to inc	# of rnds
Example 1a	86	104	18	1

Step 1: start #	86
Step 2: end #	104
Step 3: # of sts to inc	18
Step 4: # of rnds	1
Step 5: divide Step 1 by Step 3	86 ÷ 18 = 4.7
	If Step 5 is not a whole number, then find the nearest whole number below Step 1 that is.
Step 6: nearest whole number below step 1 divisible by Step 3	4 × 18 = 72
Step 7: remainder number = Step 1 – Step 6	86 – 72 = 14
Step 8: # of groups with an extra stitch	14 groups with 4 plus 1 = 14 groups with 5 sts
Step 9: # of groups with base #	(18 – 14) = 4 groups with 4 sts
Step 10: pattern	Rnd 1: [K5, m1] 14 times, [k4, m1] 4 times—104 sts.

Keeping our example numbers from the decrease section, our math will look like this:

Increase over 1 round:

e.g., In example 1a, you have 86 sts and want to increase up to 104 sts, then 104 – 86 = 18-st increase.

86 sts increased to 104 sts = 18-st inc, or working with 18 groups of sts.

86 divided by 18 = 4.7

Big Foot Knits—Andi Smith

The nearest number to 86 divisible by 18 is (18 × 4) = 72 with 14 sts remaining.
You could choose to have 14 groups of 5 sts and 4 groups of 4 sts.
Increase rnd: [K5, m1] 14 times, [k4, m1] 4 times = 104 sts.

MY SHORT INCREASE WORKSHEET (MORE COMPLEX VERSION)				
	start #	end #	# of sts to inc	# of rnds
Step 1: start #				
Step 2: end #				
Step 3: # of sts to inc				
Step 4: # of rnds				
Step 5: Step 1 divided by Step 3				
If Step 5 is not a whole number, then find the nearest whole number below Step 1 that is.				
Step 6: Nearest whole number below Step 1 divisible by Step 3				
Step 7: remainder number = Step 1 − Step 6				
Step 8: # of groups with an extra stitch				
Step 9: # of groups with base #				
Step 10: pattern				

	start #	end #	# of sts to inc	# of rnds
Example 2a	90	112	22	1

Step 1: start #	90
Step 2: end #	112
Step 3: # of sts to inc	22
Step 4: # of rnds	1
Step 5: Step 1 divided by Step 3	90 ÷ 22 = 4.09 *If Step 5 is not a whole number, then find the nearest whole number below Step 1 that is.*
Step 6: nearest whole number below 86 that is divisible by Step 3	4 × 22 = 88
Step 7: remainder number = Step 1 − Step 6	90 − 88 = 2
Step 8: # of groups with an extra stitch	22 groups − 20 = 2 groups 2 groups of 4 + 1 = 2 groups of 5

Shaping a shapely sock

Step 9: # of groups with base #	(20 – 2) = 2 groups with 4 sts
Step 10: pattern	Rnd 1: [K4, m1] 20 times, [k5, m1] 2 times—112 sts.

		start #	end #	# of sts to inc	# of rnds
Example 3b		74	108	34	2*

* You will be decreasing on 2 rounds but working a round of knit in between to equal 3 rounds.

Step 1: Start #	74
Step 2: End #	108
Step 3: # of sts to inc	34
Step 4: # of rnds	2
Step 5: Find # of sts to inc each of 2 rnds	Step 3 divided by Step 4 34 ÷ 2 = 17
Step 6: Step 1 divided by Step 5	74 ÷ 17 = 4.35 *If Step 6 is not a whole number, then find the nearest whole number below Step 1 that is.*
Step 7: Nearest whole number below 86 divisible by Step 3	4 × 17 = 68
Step 8: Remainder number = Step 1 – Step 7	74 – 68 = 6
Step 8: # of groups with an extra stitch	17 groups minus 11 = 6 groups 6 groups of 4 + 1 = 6 groups of 5
Step 9: # of groups with base #	17 – 6 = 11 groups with 4 sts
Step 10: Pattern	Rnd 1: [K4, m1] 11 times, [k5, m1] 6 times—91 sts. Rnd 2: Knit. Rnd 3: [K5, m1] 11 times, [k6, m1] 6 times—108 sts.

THE LONG INCREASE

Long increases, much like long decreases, happen over multiple rounds and are good for increasing width slowly at one or two points within the pattern. You might use this increase method, for example, on the calf of a toe-up sock or after the instep of the foot.

The math uses similar methodology to the decreases, only increasing rather than decreasing.

For example:

	start #	end #	# of sts to inc	# of rnds
Example 3c	74	108	34	34

As we can see in example 3c, we need to decrease 34 stitches over 34 rounds. I recommend working a round of straight knitting after each round of increases, as it helps the stitches retain their balance and gauge. Therefore, we will actually be making changes to 17 of the 34 rounds and ergo need to make the calculations as if we were increasing over 17 rounds rather than 34.

So, just like the above example, you have 74 stitches and want to increase to 108 stitches, for a total of 34 stitches increased.

To achieve that, we will be increasing 2 stitches in each of 17 alternate rounds.

You could choose either to work a left-leaning increase at the beginning of each alternate round paired with a right-leaning increase at the end of the round, to pair left and right increases with a couple of stitches in between, or to work a double increase at a central point.

As you've probably figured out, there are lots of variables when it comes to increases and decreases. The nice thing is that once you analyze your numbers, what you want them to do becomes quickly apparent. Use the blank worksheets at the end of each section to write in your own numbers and develop your own pattern.

Hold it all up with cuffs

In most socks, cuffs are defined as a section of ribbing that sit at the top of a sock. They're there to add a little support and elasticity. Their main function is to stop your socks from falling down. Usually comprised of very elastic stitch patterns, which help create a little extra negative ease, cuffs are generally 1½ to 2 inches in depth. Personally, I've found that over time, my cuffs tended to stretch out to their maximum width, thereby losing the elasticity they were designed for.

There are ways to help your cuffs do a better job of keeping your socks up, whilst still looking pretty:

- As noted in chapter 3, the gauge for ribbing is different than the gauge for stockinette and many lace patterns. Be sure to swatch diligently and follow the directions for finding accurate gauge. Make sure you factor in negative ease in your cuff by decreasing your stitch count by 5 or 10% as you are working out your gauge.

- Work at least a three-inch cuff. The longer columns of knit and purl stitches will more effectively grasp your leg than a short cuff.

- Use a twisted rib (see below) instead of a regular knit/purl rib, as the twisted stitch has more elasticity than a regular knit stitch.

- Begin (or end) with a good cast on (top down) or bind off (toe up)—see the Techniques appendix (page 126). A stretchy edging will lay comfortably against your skin rather than having the elastic band effect, which many of us have suffered through.

- The variety of cuff patterns available is as great as your imagination; however, a good elastic cuff is created with a combination of knit and purl stitches. Even when incorporating lace or cables into cuffs, I try and use a few knit/purl combinations between more complex stitch patterns to help keep the integrity of elasticity and support.

BASIC CUFF PATTERNS

1×1 rib (over an even number of sts)
All rounds: [K1, p1] around.

This is the most basic of rib patterns, has good stretchability and bounce back, although if the fiber blend you're knitting with is not very elastic, it can become slightly floppy and stretch out over time.

A tighter ribbing is created with twisted stitches, as follows:

Twisted rib (over an even number of sts)
All rounds: [K1tbl, p1] around.

This rib is my personal favorite—not only is it an interesting knit, but visually the columns are tight and the V's are more pronounced. This rib will keep its shape through multiple washings, will hold well on the leg, and, depending on the fiber content, will bounce back to its original shape.

2×1 rib (over a multiple of 3 sts)
All rounds: [K2, p1] around.

The 2×1 rib has more elasticity than either of the two previous ribs. Unstretched, the purl columns almost disappear; whilst stretched, the fabric almost lays flat. When worn, this rib will not offer the same support as the previous ribs.

2×2 rib (over a multiple of 4 sts)
All rounds: [K2, p2] around.

A 2×2 rib has the most elasticity of the four ribs discussed here. It maintains its elasticity when slightly stretched, but loses it if over-stretched.

Now that we know what to do with our cuffs, the numbers in our pattern can be written down like this in the following example:

SAMPLE CUFF WORKSHEET								
	stitch pattern	gauge	original circumference	# of sts	adjusted circumference	# of sts	length of cuff	# of rnds
Ex. 1	1x1 rib [k1, p1]	12 sts/18 rnds = 4"	14	12 × 14 = 168	13	12 × 13 = 156	3"	18 × 3 = 54
Ex. 1a	2x1 rib [k2, p1]	11 sts/18 rnds = 4"	14	11 × 14 = 154	13	11 × 13 = 143	3"	18 × 3 = 54

We can easily see the relevant numbers needed and work out necessary increases or decreases from the previous chapter.

(A blank cuff worksheet is printed at the end of this chapter.)

HOW TO DECREASE WITHIN A CUFF

While we want to decrease, we also want to keep as much continuity within the pattern as possible, so there are no visual breaks. By keeping the continuity of the knit and purl columns, visually these vertical lines become more aesthetically pleasing and even more flattering than broken lines.

Of course, this is again a personal preference. Just because I say it here doesn't mean that it's the knitting law. If you knit a rib that doesn't have continuous vertical lines, the yarn police will not break down your door and demand that you tink immediately and change it to what I say. They won't confiscate your stash as evidence nor will they make you wear a sign that says, Knitting Rule Breaker! This is *your* knitting. I offer suggestions and recommendations, but when it comes right down to it, it's *your* knitting to do with as you please.

Because there are limitless types of cuffs, we're not going to cover how to manipulate them all, but looking at the basic [k1, p1] rib and [k2, p2] rib will give you a good idea of how to change other types of patterns.

1×1 rib [k1, p1]

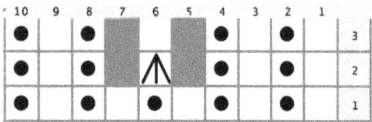

Example shown over 10 sts.
Regular Rnd: [K1, p1] 5 times.
Decrease Rnd: [K1, p1] twice, sk2p0, p1, k1, p1—8 sts.
New Regular Rnd: [K1, p1] 4 times.

By decreasing two stitches at once in the same place (the same number as the stitch pattern), we keep the basic stitch pattern in place. The mechanics of what's happening is that you're removing a full pattern repeat [k1, p1] and doing so centered around a k1, so you're taking a [k1, p1, k1] triplet and turning it into a single k1.

Alternatives: [K1, p1] becomes [k2, p1] or [k1, p2]. I like this decrease because visually, the columns appear to float into each other at the point of decrease. It's a two-stitch decrease, and adds a great visual detail when worked all across a round.

2×2 rib [k2, p2]

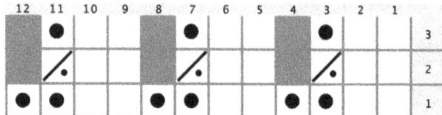

Example shown over 12 sts.
Regular Rnd: [K2, p1] around.
Decrease Rnd: [K2, p2tog] around.
New Regular Rnd: [K2, p1] around.

This type of decrease changes a p2 into a p1; visually, the knit columns continue to stand out, while the purl columns taper pleasantly without losing the integrity of the overall pattern.

Alternatives: [K2, p2] can become [k1, p2] by working a decrease over the knit stitches rather than the purl stitches. Visually, the purl columns are more prominent in this version, and the balance is thrown slightly, as the knit stitches typically stand out more than the purl stitches.

Alternative Rnd: K2, p2, k2tog, p1, [k2, p2] to end of rnd.

HOW TO INCREASE WITHIN A CUFF

Sometimes, the height of our sock makes the cuff fall in a place where your leg circumference increases by more than an inch or so. If we don't change the number of stitches within the cuff to reflect that change, then the cuffs won't fit properly. The negative ease within the cuff will change and make them less effective at doing the job they're designed to do (namely, keeping your sock up!). Of course, if it's a slight change (an inch or less), it's perfectly fine to carry on as normal. However, for those times when the start of our cuff has a 2" differential than that at the end of the cuff, increases are in order.

In the examples shown below, I've listed m1 or m2 as an indication of increase. The method you use to increase is up to you.

1×1 rib increase

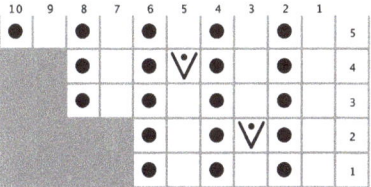

Example shown over 6 sts.
Regular Rnd: [K1, p1] around.
Increase Rnd 1: K1, p1, (k1, p1, k1) into next stitch, p1, k1, p1—8 sts.
Next Rnd: [K1, p1] around.
Increase Rnd 2: [K1, p1] twice, (k1, p1, k1) into next stitch, p1, k1, p1—10 sts.
New Regular Rnd: [K1, p1] around.

Visually, this increase flows a new knit stitch out of an existing one—a great design detail.

2×2 rib increase

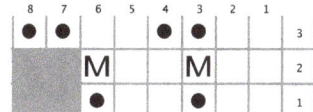

In this example, we begin with a [k2, p1] stitch pattern and end with a [k2, p2] pattern. However, you could start with a [k2, p2] and increase to a [k3, p2] or a [k2, p3]. The choice is yours.

Example shown over 6 sts.
Regular Rnd: [K2, p1] around.
Increase Rnd: [K2, pfb] twice—8 sts.
New Regular Rnd: [K2, p2] around.

How you choose to manipulate your stitch count is up to you. Swatch up some ribbing, add increases and decreases and see what is visually pleasing to you.

MY CUFF WORKSHEET							
stitch pattern	gauge	circumference inches start	# of sts	circumference inches end	# of sts	length of cuff	# of rnds

The well-heeled sock

As in all aspects of knitting, there are many different methods for knitting heels. Whether you work top down or toe up, you can work a heel flap, afterthought, or short row heel, along with many other varieties.

However, for the purposes of this book, I'm going to concentrate on afterthought heels. This is my favorite type of heel because it allows you to continue your sock without taking a break in the stitch pattern. It produces a heel that is comfortable, is very easy to knit, and to my eye is the most visually pleasing. That said, you can always take the principles I talk about here and apply them to other types of heel.

The only thing I feel is missing from an afterthought heel is a gusset, that triangular piece of fabric that is often put into socks on either side of the heel to add width and to create more ease as your leg transitions into your foot. However, because we are altering the circumference of our socks frequently, I have worked the gusset—or rather, the width added by a gusset—into the body of the sock instead so that a traditional gusset isn't needed.

To prepare for a basic afterthought heel, work to where your foot and leg meet. Knit the stitches for the heel with waste yarn, then slip the stitches you just worked back onto your left-hand needle and knit them again with your main yarn. Carry on knitting the sock as usual. Once you have finished the toe, come back to place the stitches that are on waste yarn back onto your needles to work the heel (see next section).

The width of the heel on any given sock can be either the standard 50% of stitches, or more or less, depending on two things: the flow of the stitch pattern and the shape of your heel.

Because an afterthought heel is constructed in basically the same way as a top-down toe, you can vary the shape of the heel to match the shape of your foot. Shallow or deep, narrow or wide, a deep curved decrease or a squarer shape, choose what works for you. Below, I've charted some basic heel types that you can use, but get adventurous and use the blank charts to make your own.

The types of heel I've worked within this book are all ones where you divide your stitches into two sections, and work a long decrease along either edge of the two sections. I like to move the long decrease line from the second stitch of the beginning/end of my two sections over to the 4th or 5th stitch. This creates a more curved pocket than a standard heel flap so that it cups your heel shape more snugly.

When you are working out the math for your sock worksheet and have different stitch counts than a generic sock, be sure to increase or decrease before your afterthought heel placement so that you have the correct-to-you number of stitches to fit your heel.

HOW TO KNIT AN AFTERTHOUGHT HEEL

Pick up the stitches from the waste yarn and divide them onto two needles, so that the stitches for your leg are on one needle and the stitches for your heel are on another. If you are a devotee of double-pointed needles, then a good rule of thumb is to place half the stitches from either the leg or sock onto one needle, the other half onto a second and all the remaining stitches onto a third. This way you can easily see where your decreases need to be.

Unpick the waste yarn a few stitches at a time, placing live stitches onto needles. Knit one round, picking up and knitting two or three stitches in the gaps between needles. Being sure to divide stitches evenly, make the heel by using one of the following heel types.

A note on heel charts

You will see that all the charts have 20 rounds—about 2" long depending on your gauge and 70 stitches wide (divided into 2 or 35 sts each side). Work out how many rounds you need by multiplying the measurement by number of rounds per inch in your gauge. Add rounds by working extra plain rounds between shaping.

SAMPLE HEEL DEPTH WORKSHEET			
	Sally	**Celeste**	**Betty**
rnds-per-inch gauge, including negative ease	10 rnds per inch	9 rnds per inch	9 rnds per inch
heel depth (G from measuring chart)	3"	2.5"	3"
gauge × depth = total # of rnds	10 × 3 = 33 rnds	9 × 2.5 = 22.5 or 22 rnds	9 × 3 = 27 rnds

As we can see from the worksheet above, our three intrepid knitters each have different measurements, so the number of rounds each needs to knit for their heel will be different from each other.

MY HEEL DEPTH WORKSHEET	
rnds-per-inch gauge, including negative ease	
heel depth (G from measuring chart)	
gauge × G = total # of rnds	

The charts in this chapter are drawn with 35 stitches each, or 70 stitches total. This is an arbitrary number, of course, since it would be impossible for me to create charts within this book for every stitch number.

HOW TO CREATE YOUR OWN CHART

Use the blank chart on the next page to create your personal heel chart.

1. Draw straight lines to define your stitch and round count.
2. Refer back to the chart that depicts your heel icon and copy the shape within your chart, making it wider, narrower, taller or shorter depending on *your* stitch and round counts.
3. Don't worry if your increase/decrease count is different from mine. As long as you keep to the shape and basic spacing of them, you will get a well-fitting heel.
4. Practice. Practice makes perfect. Work a couple of heel samples and try them on. Make adjustments as necessary. Once you have the perfect heel pocket, you'll be able to use it for every pair of socks you ever make!

THE STANDARD HEEL

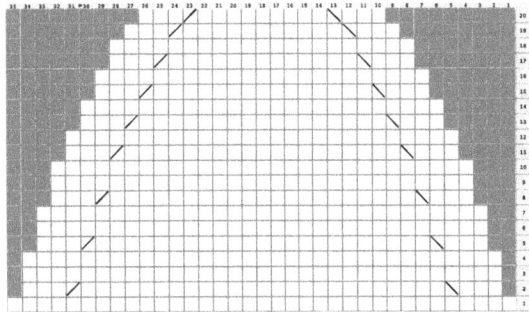

The standard heel pattern creates the type of pocket you'd find in most afterthought heel patterns. It's traditionally trapezoidal in shape, with a slight curve at the narrow end.

Rnds 1, 3, 4, 6, 7, 9, 10, 12, 14, 16, 18: Knit.
Rnd 2: [K3, ssk, k25, k2tog, k3] twice.
Rnd 5: [K3, ssk, k23, k2tog, k3] twice.
Rnd 8: [K3, ssk, k21, k2tog, k3] twice.
Rnd 11: [K3, ssk, k19, k2tog, k3] twice.
Rnd 13: [K3, ssk, k17, k2tog, k3] twice.
Rnd 15: [K3, ssk, k15, k2tog, k3] twice.
Rnd 17: [K3, ssk, k13, k2tog, k3] twice.
Rnd 19: [K3, ssk, k11, k2tog, k3] twice.
Rnd 20: [K3, ssk, k9, k2tog, k3] twice.

Join rem sts using either kitchener stitch or a three-needle bind off.

THE SQUARE HEEL

If your heel and ankle don't taper in, then this is the heel type for you. This pattern gives you coverage without creating a too-tight pocket.

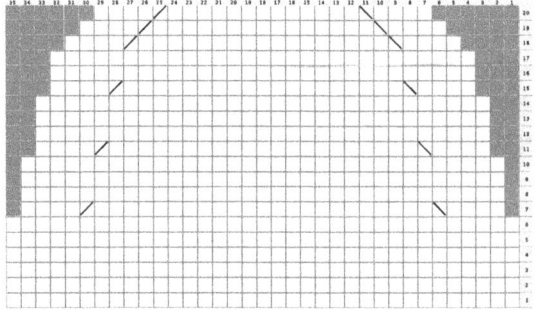

Rnds 1–6, 8–10, 12–14, 16–17: Knit.
Rnd 7: [K4, ssk, k23, k2tog, k4] twice.
Rnd 11: [K4, ssk, k21, k2tog, k4] twice.
Rnd 15: [K4, ssk, k19, k2tog, k4] twice.
Rnd 18: [K4, ssk, k17, k2tog, k4] twice.
Rnd 19: [K4, ssk, k15, k2tog, k4] twice.
Rnd 20: [K4, ssk, k13, k2tog, k4] twice.

Join rem sts using either kitchener stitch or a three-needle bind off.

THE POINTY HEEL

If your heel is narrower than the rest of your foot and the back of your ankle tapers more than an inch, then a pointy heel is the way to go.

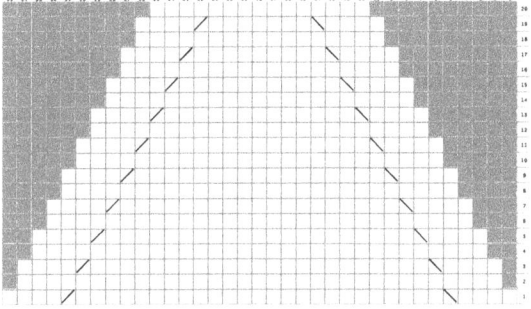

Rnd 1 (and all odd rnds): Knit.
Rnd 2: [K2, ssk, k27, k2tog, k2] twice.
Rnd 4: [K2, ssk, k25, k2tog, k2] twice.
Rnd 6: [K2, ssk, k23, k2tog, k2] twice.

Continue working in this fashion, knitting 1 rnd, then decreasing at the 4 points established every alternate rnd, until 20 rnds have been completed.

Join rem sts using either kitchener stitch or a three-needle bind off.

As I've mentioned before, this really isn't an exact science. You have to find what type of heel pocket works for your individual foot. It could be that you have to re-work your heel until you hit on the perfect combination of decreases that fit your shape, however, it's worth the time and effort to do so to obtain that perfect fit.

BLANK HEEL CHART

Room for toes

In most sock patterns, the toe shaping creates either a trapezoidal flap or a spiraling pocket. However, these shapes suit few, if any, feet. After embarrassing myself by asking lots of strangers, friends, and family members to share their toes with me, I came up with five basic toe types: left-sloping, right-sloping, curved, square, and tapered out. Not a trapezoid in sight! As much as I loved knitting the standard top-down toe, it seemed it wasn't the best fit for tootsies!

If you think about it, we really need the toes to fit better than anything else on the sock. Our poor toes are wrapped tightly inside shoes for most of the day, so if there's extra fabric at the tip of your sock, it's going to become uncomfortable, cause blisters, or worse, become over-worn and fray! (In my humble opinion, a hole in hand-knitted socks is much worse than a blister!) Similarly, too little fabric on the toe over-stretches, causing similar problems. So it behooves us to spend some time finding the best-fitting toe pocket for each of us.

Once I started knitting a toe pocket that was shaped like my actual toes, I was surprised by just how much more comfortable my socks became.

ANALYZE YOUR TOES

In chapter 2, you worked out what toe type you are. Now it's time to translate that type into a knittable toe for your socks.

The essential measurement that you will need is the distance between the point where your little toe starts to curve and the tip of your highest toe.

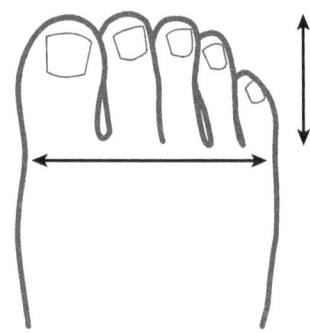

Now look at the depth of your toes. How high off the ground does your big toe nail sit? A half inch? An inch? If we reflect that height in our shaping method, our pocket will truly be more toe-shaped. For example, if your toe depth is ½", and your stitch gauge is 8 stitches per inch, then by moving the shapings to 4 stitches in, that shaping will glide over the actual top and bottom of your toes. If your toe depth is ¾", then move the shapings to the 6th stitch position.

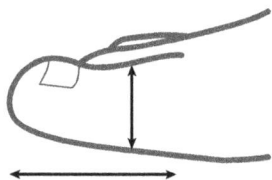

Moving those shapings to where the shape actually occurs on your toes will create a toe pocket that hugs the end of your foot.

I like to include extra increases/decreases on the first (toe up) or last (top down) round to add extra shaping to the toe pocket, but don't be bound by my preferences. Experiment and make your own!

BASIC PATTERN FOR DIFFERENT TOE TYPES

The charts and patterns below are worked over 2 × 35 sts and 20 rounds. Obviously, this is an arbitrary number and it may well be that your stitch and/or round count will be different.

SAMPLE TOE ROUND WORKSHEET			
	Sally	Celeste	Betty
rnds-per-inch gauge	10 rnds/inch	9 rnds/inch	9 rnds/inch
measurement C from measuring worksheet	1.5"	2.75"	2.5"
gauge × C = # of rnds in toe	10 × 1.5 = 15 rnds	9 × 2.75 = 25.75 or 25 rnds (rounded down)	9 × 2.5 = 22.5 or 23 rnds (rounded up)

MY TOE ROUND WORKSHEET	
rnds-per-inch gauge	
measurement C from measuring worksheet	
gauge × C = # of rnds in toe	

Use the blank charts at the end of this chapter to create your personal toe chart.

1. Draw straight lines to define your stitch and round count.
2. Refer back to the chart in this chapter that depicts your toe icon and copy the shape within your chart, making it wider, narrower, taller, or shorter depending on *your* stitch and round counts.
3. Don't worry if your increase/decrease count is different from mine. As long as you keep to the shape and basic spacing of them, you will get a well-fitting toe.
4. Practice. Practice makes perfect. Work a couple of toe samples and try them on. Make adjustments as necessary. Once you have the perfect toe pocket, you'll be able to use it for every pair of socks you ever make!

The pattern is written with the assumption that you are working with two needles and that the front of your sock on the first needle and the back on the second. If you work with double-pointed needles, be sure to configure your stitch counts accordingly.

Regardless of the number of stitches on your needles, basic shapings will all follow the same decrease/increase pattern, unless you want them shorter, longer, or wider. It's really up to you. These are basic templates just waiting for your individual footprint.

TOP-DOWN LEFT SLOPE

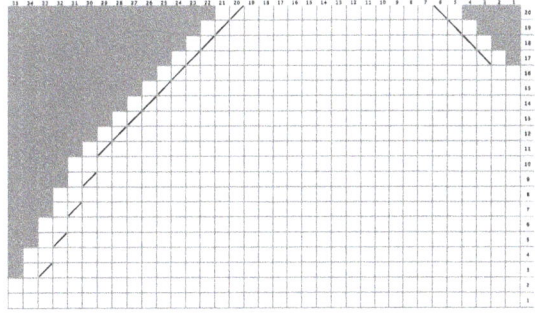

Rnds 1, 2, 4, 6, 8, 10: Knit.
Rnd 3: Needle 1: K32, k2tog, k1. Needle 2: K1, ssk, k32.
Rnd 5: Needle 1: K31, k2tog, k1. Needle 2: K1, ssk, k31.

Rnd 7: Needle 1: K30, k2tog, k1. Needle 2: K1, ssk, k30.
Rnd 9: Needle 1: K29, k2tog, k1. Needle 2: K1, ssk, k29.
Rnd 11: Needle 1: K28, k2tog, k1. Needle 2: K1, ssk, k28.
Rnd 12: Needle 1: K27, k2tog, k1. Needle 2: K1, ssk, k27.
Rnd 13: Needle 1: K26, k2tog, k1. Needle 2: K1, ssk, k26.
Rnd 14: Needle 1: K25, k2tog, k1. Needle 2: K1, ssk, k25.
Rnd 15: Needle 1: K24, k2tog, k1. Needle 2: K1, ssk, k24.
Rnd 16: Needle 1: K23, k2tog, k1. Needle 2: K1, ssk, k23.
Rnd 17: Both needles: K1, ssk, k19, k2tog, k1.
Rnd 18: Both needles: K1, ssk, k17, k2tog, k1.
Rnd 19: Both needles: K1, ssk, k15, k2tog, k1.
Rnd 20: Both needles: K1, ssk, k13, k2tog, k1—17 sts rem on each needle (34 sts total).

Join rem sts using either kitchener stitch or a three-needle bind off.

TOE-UP LEFT SLOPE

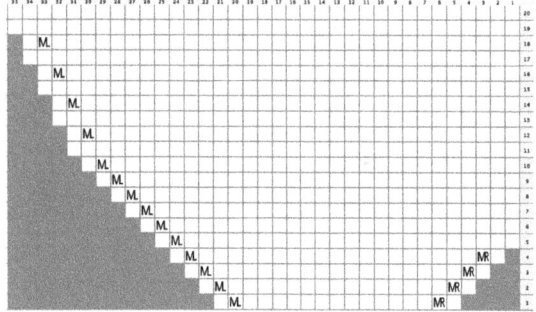

CO 34 sts using your preferred method and divide over 2 needles (17 on each needle).

Rnd 1: Both needles: K1, m1R, knit to last 2 sts, m1L, k1—19 sts on each needle (38 sts total).
Rnds 2, 3 & 4: Both needles: K1, m1R, knit to last 2 sts, m1L, k2.
Rnds 5–10: Needle 1: Knit to last 2 sts, m1L, k1. Needle 2: K1, m1R, knit to end.
Rnds 11, 13, 15, 17, 19 & 20: Knit.

Rnds 12, 14, 16 & 18: Needle 1: Knit to last 2 sts, m1R, k1. Needle 2: K1, m1L, knit to end.
Continue knitting sock.

TOP-DOWN RIGHT SLOPE

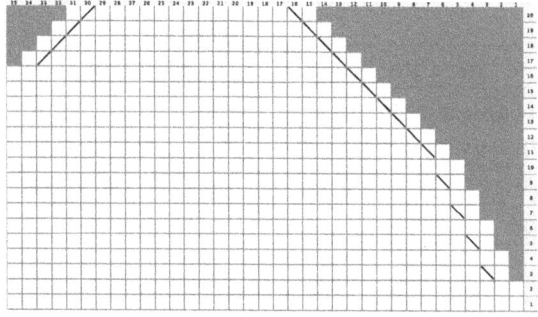

Rnds 1, 2, 4, 6, 8 & 10: Knit.
Rnds 3, 5, 7, 9 & 11–16: Needle 1: K1, ssk, knit to end of needle. Needle 2: Knit to last 3 sts, k2tog, k1.
Rnds 17–20: Both needles: K1, ssk, knit to last 3 sts on needle, k2tog, k1.

Join rem sts using either kitchener stitch or a three-needle bind off.

TOE-UP RIGHT SLOPE

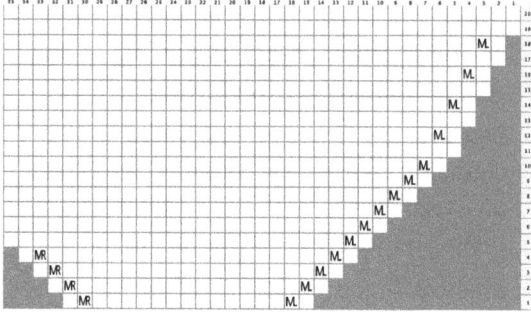

CO 34 sts using your preferred method and divide over 2 needles (17 on each needle).

Rnds 1–4: Both needles: K1, m1L, knit to last 2 sts, m1R, k1.
Rnds 5–10, 12, 14, 16 & 18: Needle 1: K1, m1L, knit to end of needle, k1. Needle 2: Knit to last 2 sts, m1R, K1.
Rnds 11, 13, 15, 17, 19 & 20: Knit.
Continue knitting sock.

TOP-DOWN CURVED

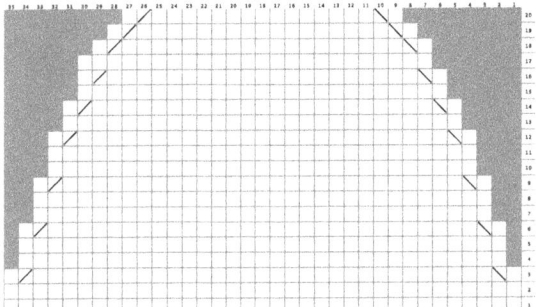

Right and left toes are the same, and both needles are worked the same.

Rnds 1, 2, 4, 5, 7, 8, 10, 11, 13 & 15: Knit.
Rnds 3, 6, 9, 12, 14 & 16–20: K1, ssk, knit to last 3 sts on needle, k2tog, k1.

Join rem sts using either kitchener stitch or a three-needle bind off.

TOE-UP CURVED

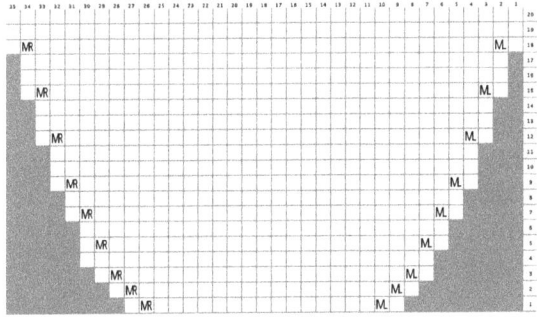

Right and left toes are the same, and both needles are worked the same.

CO 34 sts using your preferred method and divide over 2 needles (17 on each needle).

Rnds 1–5, 7, 9, 12, 15 & 18: K1, m1L, knit to last 2 sts, m1R, k1.
All other rnds: Knit.
Continue knitting sock.

TOP-DOWN SQUARE

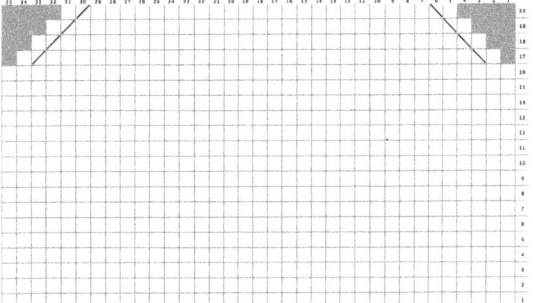

Right and left toes are the same, and both needles are worked the same.

Rnds 1–15: Knit.
Rnds 16–20: K1, ssk, knit to last 3 sts, k2tog, k1.

Join rem sts using either kitchener stitch or a three-needle bind off.

TOE-UP SQUARE

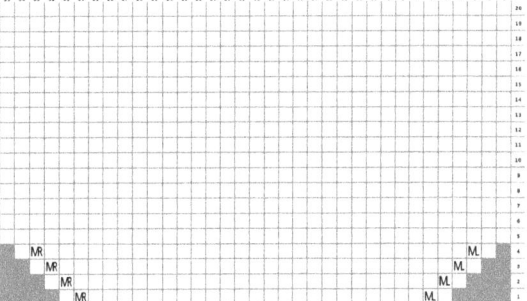

Right and left toes are the same, and both needles are worked the same.

CO 54 sts using your preferred method and divide over 2 needles (27 on each needle).

Rnds 1–4: K1, m1L, knit to last 2 sts, m1R, k1.
Rnds 5–20: Knit.
Continue knitting sock.

TOP-DOWN TAPERED

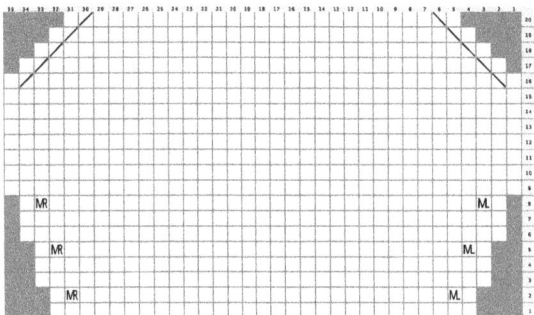

Right and left toes are the same, and both needles are worked the same.

Rnds 1–5, 7–9, 11, 13–16: Knit.
Rnds 6, 10 & 12: K1, m1R, knit to last 2 sts, m1L, k1.
Rnds 17–20: K1, ssk, knit to last 3 sts, k2tog, k1.

Join rem sts using either kitchener stitch or a three-needle bind off.

TOE-UP TAPERED

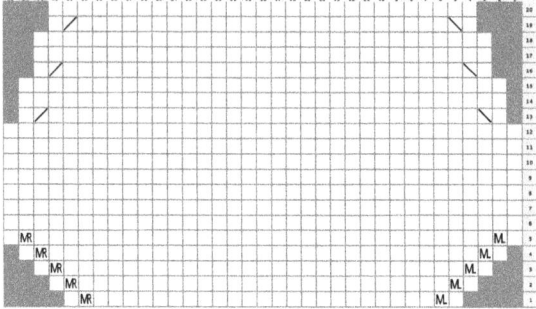

Right and left toes are the same, and both needles are worked the same.

CO 54 sts using your preferred method and divide over 2 needles (27 on each needle).

Rnds 1–4: K1, m1L, knit to last 2 sts, m1R, k1.
Rnds 5–8, 10, 12–14, 16–20: Knit.
Rnds 9, 11 & 15: K1, ssk, knit to last 3 sts, k2tog, k1.
Continue knitting sock.

༄ ༄ ༄

And that's really all there is to toes. Find a shape that works for you and replicate it within your stitch and round count. Hopefully, the shapes I've provided will give you a good starting point to create your own individual toe shapes.

BLANK TOE CHART

Types of toes

LEFT AND RIGHT SLOPE

CURVED

TAPERED

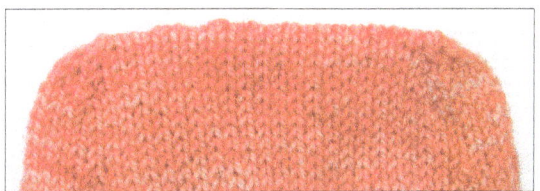

SQUARE

Your own custom-fit sock

You now have all the information you need to knit the perfect stockinette sock for *you*. The good news is that to do the math and analyze all those numbers only takes about an hour.

Below, I've collected all the mini worksheets from the preceding chapters. Spend some time on the worksheets, and, as you're working, slot numbers into your master pattern sheet. Don't be alarmed if you don't need every section of every worksheet. Use what you need to find those magic pattern numbers and forget the rest.

CUSTOM TOE-UP SOCK WORKSHEET	
cast-on method	
toe type	
stitch gauge	
row gauge	
# of sts in toe start	
# of rnds in toe end	
# of rnds in foot	
incs/decs	
# of sts in afterthought heel prep rnd	
leg type	
# of rnds in leg	
incs/decs	
cuff pattern	
rnds in cuff	
incs/decs	
bind-off method	
heel type	
# of rnds in heel	
heel chart	

CUSTOM TOP-DOWN SOCK WORKSHEET	
leg type	
cast-on method	
cuff pattern	
cuff gauge	
# of sts to cast on	
# of rnds in cuff	
incs/decs	
stockinette gauge	
# of sts in leg	
# of rnds in leg	
incs/decs	
heel type	
# of sts in afterthought heel prep rnd	
# of rnds in foot	
incs/decs	
toe type	
# of rnds in toe	
toe chart	
bind off method	
# of rnds in heel	
heel chart	

And there you have it: your very own custom sock pattern, created by you to fit you.

Beyond basic stockinette

Now that you've mastered creating your own custom stockinette sock, it's time to look at adding stitch patterns, whether they are cables, lace, or twisted stitches.

Each of the following sock patterns are specifically designed to be adapted. By having columns of pattern grouped with columns of stockinette or reverse stockinette, I've created a place within each sock to effect change without changing the pattern detail. Long and short increases and decreases (see page 27) can be worked within any of these patterns, so the techniques you've learned in previous chapters can be applied here.

All the patterns are appropriate for all the different types of leg and foot shapes. The first three listed are very easily manipulated, whilst the remaining ones are easily manipulated, but may take a little thinking through before you dive in.

In each pattern, I give you the basics of the pattern, both for top-down and toe-up construction, then show you how to modify each one.

Just like when you swatched for your stockinette sock, knitting a gauge swatch is an essential step toward creating a well-fitting patterned sock.

As with your stockinette swatch, you'll need to work with the same needles and yarn that you will use for your prospective patterned sock.

THE SWATCH PATTERN

Because we'll be using both the stitch pattern and a column of stockinette or reverse stockinette combined, we need to swatch both of them together to see how they relate to each other visually as well as to find an accurate round and stitch gauge.

That said, I've found that swatching the stitch pattern with a group of at least 3 stitches between each pattern works best. You may choose 3 knit stitches, a triplet of p1, k1, p1, or 3 purl stitches if your pattern is based on a reverse stockinette field.

The number of stitches and rounds that you need in your swatch totally depends on how many stitches are in your stitch pattern and how many stitches you initially insert between your pattern fields, as well as the number of rounds in the pattern repeat.

To get a good representation of your patterns for measuring, I recommend working at least 2 repeats of rounds and 4 repeats of stitches, or at least 40 stitches and rounds.

For example:

	example 1	example 2	example 3
# of sts in stitch patt	7	12	8
# of sts between	3	4	3
# of rnds in each patt repeat	12	32	10
# of stitch reps	4	4	4
# of rnd reps	3	2	4
# of sts to cast on	(7 + 3) × 4 = 40 sts	(12 + 4) × 4 = 64 sts	(8 + 3) × 4 = 44 sts
# of rnds to work	12 × 3 = 36 rnds	32 × 2 = 64 rnds	10 × 4 = 40 rnds

As you can see, the stitch and round count vary depending on the number of stitches and rounds in the base stitch pattern. Yours will be different for each pattern and swatch.

MY STITCH PATTERN SWATCH WORKSHEET	
# of sts in stitch patt	
# of sts between	
# of rnds in each patt repeat	
# of stitch reps	
# of rnd reps	
# of sts to cast on	
# of rnds to work	

Work the swatch in the same way as a stockinette swatch by casting on with a good stretchy cast on, work the necessary rounds and then bind off in a similarly stretchy method. Block and measure your swatch the same as your stockinette swatch.

Both the stitch pattern and rib gauge should be swatched separately.

MY STITCH PATTERN GAUGE WORKSHEET	
yarn	
needles	
stitch pattern	
sts per inch	
negative ease %	
gauge	
sts per inch minus negative ease	

MY RIB GAUGE WORKSHEET	
yarn	
needles	
stitch pattern	
sts per inch	
negative ease %	
gauge	
sts per inch minus negative ease	

In each of the following patterns, I give measurements and sizing for three different base sizes based on *my* gauge. If you wish to use those numbers, be sure that your gauge matches the one listed. If you wish to work at your own gauge, the sizing will be different to that listed, and you'll have to work out the number of pattern repeats you need that will fit in your circumferences.

To do this, practice swatching with different numbers of stitches between the main stitch pattern until you find one that will work with your individual numbers.

To determine which of the three sizes you need to knit, find the smallest circumference on your chart and add stitches to the pattern accordingly. That way, when you are working with the smallest number of stitches within your pattern, you'll still have full pattern repeats.

Remember: you may need to add or decrease stitches within your pattern. Chart out your changes on graph paper before you start.

THE PATTERNS

Pavarti

This powerful Hindu goddess of love, devotion, and benevolence was the wife of Shiva. Pavarti had over 100 different incarnations, each with its own personality, making this the perfect name for a sock that can be manipulated and changed as many different ways as there are feet. The purled background both offers the perfect counterfoil for a pretty V-shaped lace, and also affords us the ideal place to change up our stitch counts. Whether you choose to use long or short increases and decreases, they'll blend wonderfully into the purls. In this design, be sure to work purl rather than knit increases and decreases for a truly seamless look.

MATERIALS

Knit Picks Stroll (75% superwash merino wool, 25% nylon; 231 yds/211m per 50g ball), 2 balls; sample uses Agate Heather colorway

US #1.5/2.5mm needles for working in the round: dpns, 2 short circulars, or 1 longer circular

Cable needle
About 2 yds of cotton waste yarn in a similar weight

SIZE & FIT

Foot circumference: 10.5 (12.25, 14)"
Sample shown in smallest size with no increases in the leg or foot.

GAUGE

Pattern repeat (11 sts wide × 12 rnds high) = 1.75" wide × 1" high

Both versions: cuff

Cuff Pattern

11	10	9	8	7	6	5	4	3	2	1	
•	•					•	•		•	•	8
•	•					•	•		•	•	7
•	•					•	•		•	•	6
•	•					•	•		•	•	5
•	•					•	•		•	•	4
•	•					•	•		•	•	3
•	•					•	•		•	•	2
•	•					•	•		•	•	1

Top-down version

Pavarti Top-Down Stitch Pattern

11	10	9	8	7	6	5	4	3	2	1	
•	•	•				•	•	•	•	•	12
•	•	•				•	•	•	•	•	11
•	•	•				•	•	•	•	•	10
•	•	•	<->		<->	•	•	•	•	•	9
•	•	/	O		O	\	•	•	•	•	8
•	•						•	•	•	•	7
•	/	O				O	\	•	•	•	6
•								•	•	•	5
/	O						O	\	•	•	4
•	•	•	<->		<->	•	•	•	•	•	3
•	•	•				•	•	•	•	•	2
•	•	•				•	•	•	•	•	1

Symbol	Meaning	Symbol	Meaning
•	purl	\	ssk
(blank)	knit	O	yo
<->	3 st wrap	/	k2tog

PAVARTI TOP-DOWN WORKSHEET			
cast-on method	Choose your preferred cast-on method.		
circumference	10.5 inches	12.25 inches	14 inches
# of sts to cast on	66 sts	77 sts	88 sts
# of rnds per inch	12 rnds per inch		
length of cuff	3 inches	3 inches	3.5 inches
# of rnds in cuff	36 rnds	36 rnds	42 rnds
# of sts in leg	66 sts	77 sts	88 sts
leg length	Use your own leg length.		
# of rnds in leg	Work out your own # of rnds by multiplying leg length by 12 (number of rnds per inch).		
# of sts for afterthought heel	31 sts	38 sts	42 sts
foot pattern	Work across 33 sts in patt as set, p2. This sets the patt for the 35 instep sts. Knit rem 31 sts of round with waste yarn; return to start of those sts, knit them again. From here, continue as set, working across instep in patt and knitting sole sts.	End final leg rnd 2 sts before end of rnd. Knit 2, work 3 reps of patt, then p2, k2. These 39 sts are for the top of your foot. Knit rem 38 sts with waste yarn and then re-knit them with project yarn. Continue to work front of sock in patt with the added k2 at the beg and ending with a p2, k2, and knit the 38 sts of the sole.	Arrange sts so that front of sock begins at the start of a patt rep, work 4 reps and an extra p2 (46 sts) Knit rem 42 sts with waste yarn and then re-knit them with project yarn. Continue to work front of sock in patt and ending with a p2 and knit the sole of your sock.
length of foot minus toe	Use your own foot length.		
# of rnds in foot	Multiply foot length by rnds per inch (12).		
toe type			
toe	Divide the sts so you have 2 equal groups. If you have an odd number, add an extra decrease to one of the groups as you start your decrease pattern. Follow the toe pattern that best fits your toe (see chapter 7).		
closure method	Join rem toe sts using kitchener stitch or 3-needle bind off.		
heel	Pick up heel sts and work the heel of your choice.		

Toe-up version

Pavarti Toe-Up Stitch Pattern

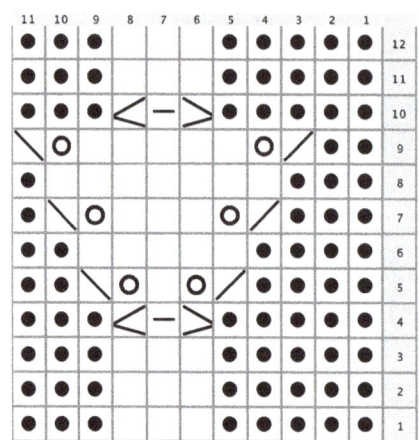

Modifying the pattern

If we take another look at the top-down chart for Pavarti, we can see that columns 1 and 2 never change:

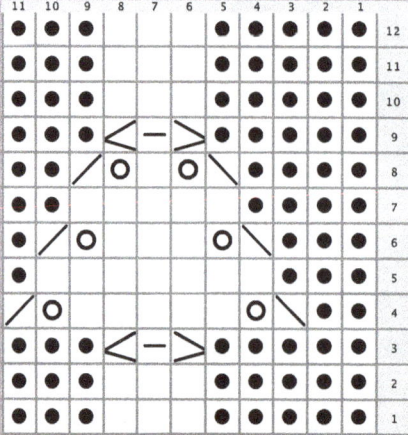

These columns are therefore the perfect place from which to add or subtract stitches. If you were to add 1 stitch to column 2 on Rnds 3, 6 and 9, then your stitch counts would increase thus:

# of patt reps in sock	Rnd 3	Rnd 6	Rnd 9
6	66 + 6 = 72 sts	72 + 6 = 78 sts	78 + 6 = 84 sts
7	77 +7 = 84 sts	84 +7 = 91 sts	91 sts + 7 = 98 sts
8	88 + 8 = 96 sts	96 + 8 = 104 sts	104 + 8 = 112 sts

How and where you manipulate the stitch count is entirely dependent on the numbers you need—but notice how easy it is to make a change without altering the basic pattern.

PAVARTI TOE-UP WORKSHEET			
cast on	Choose your preferred cast-on method.		
circumference	10.5 inches	12.25 inches	14 inches
# of rnds per inch	12 rnds per inch		
toe	Work a toe that ends with 66 sts.	Work a toe that ends with 77 sts.	Work a toe that ends with 88 sts.
foot pattern	Arrange sts so that you are starting at the beginning of a patt rep and work 35 sts ending with p2 for front of sock, and knit rem 31 sts with waste yarn, and then again with project yarn. Continue to work the front of your sock in pattern with a p2 at the end, and knit the 31 sts that make up the sole of your foot.	Arrange the sts so that you start 2 sts before a complete stitch pattern, Knit 2, work 3 reps of pattern, then p2, k2. These 39 sts are for the top of your foot. Knit the rem 38 sts with waste yarn and then re-knit them with project yarn. Continue to work the front of your sock in pattern with the added k2 at the beginning and ending with a p2,k2, and knit the 38 sts of the sole.	Arrange the sts so that the front of your sock begins at the start of a pattern repeat, work 4 reps and an extra p2 (46 sts) Knit the rem 42 sts with waste yarn and then re-knit them with project yarn. Continue to work the front of your sock in pattern and ending with a p2 and knit the sole of your sock.
foot length	Use your own foot length.		
# of rnds in foot	Work out your own # of rnds by multiplying foot length by 12 (number of rnds per inch).		
# of sts for afterthought heel	31 sts	38 sts	42 sts
leg length	Use your own leg length.		
# of rnds in leg	Leg length multiplied by rnd gauge (12).		
leg pattern	Arrange sts so that the front of your sock now starts at the start of a stitch pattern and work complete reps of the st patt across the entire rnd.		
cuff length	3"	3"	3"
# of rnds in cuff	36 rnds	36 rnds	42 rnds
bind off	Work Jeny's Surprisingly Stretchy Bind Off.		
afterthought heel	Pick up heel sts and work the heel of your choice.		

Marama

Marama was the female personification of the moon in Maori culture. She was also the goddess of weaving, plaiting, and the arts. Just as the moon's presence weaves in and out of our lives every month, so too does the cable in this sock by weaving in and out to create a stunning detail.

MATERIALS

Sanguine Gryphon Skinny Bugga! (80% superwash merino, 10% cashmere, 10% nylon; 424 yds / 388m per 113g skein), 1 skein; samples use Gunmetal and Swift Long-Winged Skinner

**Sanguine Gryphon is no longer trading under that name, but has separated into Cephalopod Yarns and The Verdant Gryphon. Both companies continue to carry Skinny Bugga!

US #1.5/2.5mm needles for working in the round: dpns, 2 short circulars or 1 longer circular

2 stitch markers
Cable needle
About 2 yds of waste cotton yarn in a similar weight

SIZE & FIT

Average foot circumference: 10 (12, 14)"
Average leg circumference: 10 (12, 14)"
Samples shown in smallest size.

GAUGE

Cable section 3.5" wide on the leg × 28 sts, 1.75" wide on the foot × 16 sts worked in the round

24 sts/44 rnds = 4"/10cm St st worked in the round

Top-down version

Work Rnds 1 & 2 of top-down cuff chart 15 times, then work Rnd 3 once.

Work complete Marama Leg Cable chart (Rnds 1–67).

Set up afterthought heel.

Work complete Marama Left or Right Cable Foot chart (Rnds 1–72).

Work toe as described in top-down worksheet.

Toe-up version

Work toe as described in toe-up worksheet.

Work complete Marama Left or Right Cable Foot chart (Rnds 1–72).

Set up afterthought heel.

Work complete Marama Leg Cable chart (Rnds 1–67).

Work Rnd 1 of toe-up cuff chart once, then Rnds 2 & 3 fifteen times.

Big Foot Knits—Andi Smith

Top-down cuff pattern

Toe-up cuff pattern

	knit knit stitch
•	purl purl stitch
	c2 over 1 right P sl1 to CN, hold in back. k2, p1 from CN
	c2 over 1 left P sl2 to CN, hold in front. p1, k2 from CN
	c2 over 2 right sl2 to CN, hold in back. k2, k2 from CN
	c2 over 2 left sl 2 to CN, hold in front. k2, k2 from CN
	c2 over 2 left P sl 2 to CN, hold in front. p2, k2 from CN
	c2 over 2 right P sl2 to CN, hold in back. k2, p2 from CN

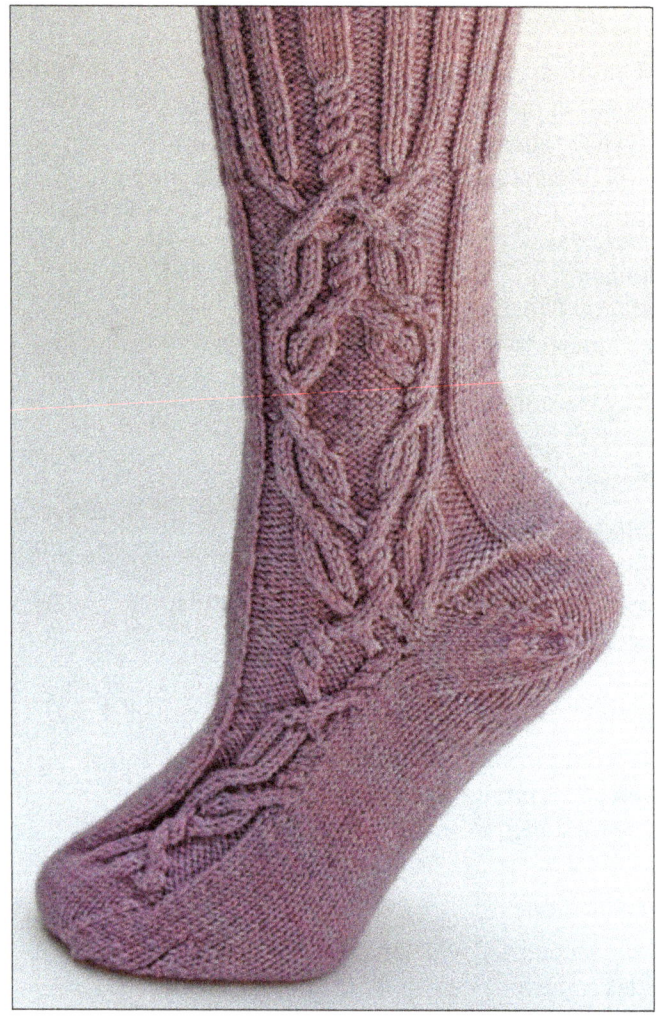

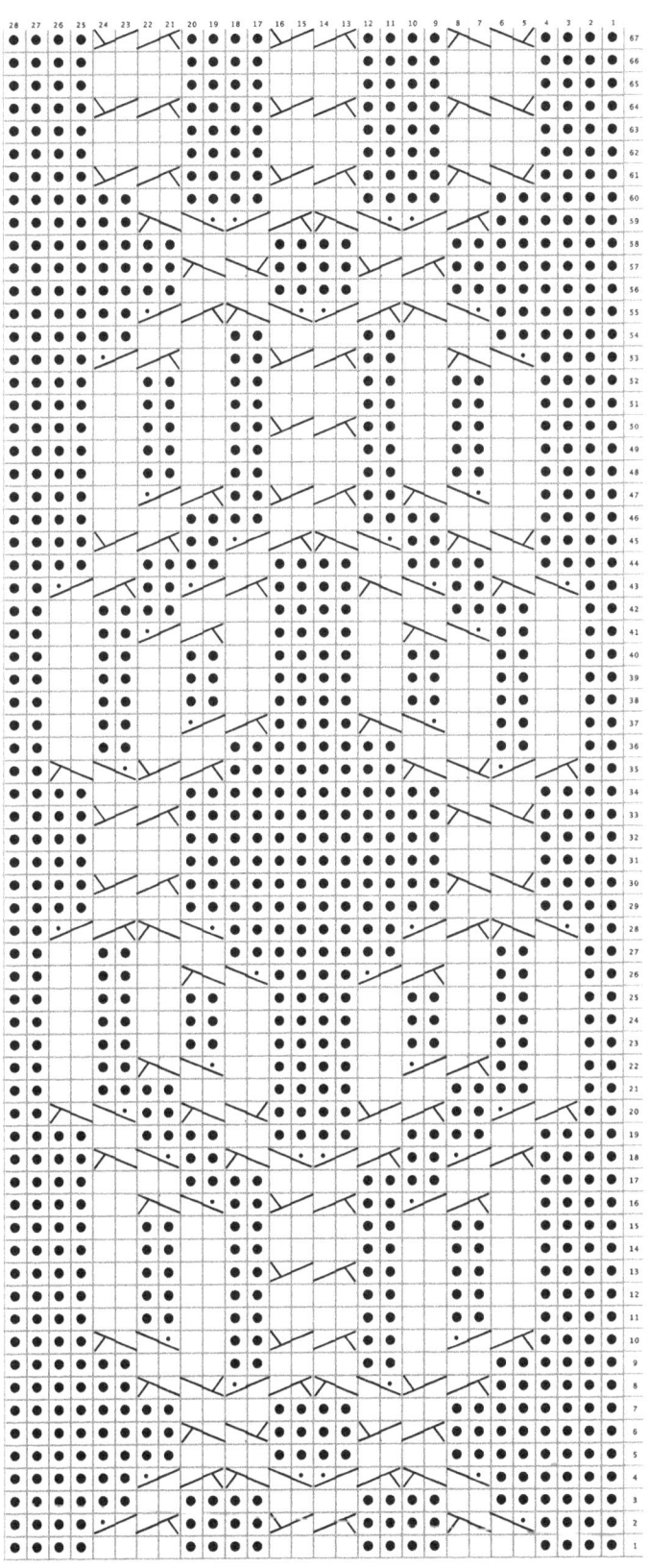

Marama Leg
Cable pattern

For this sock, all leg and foot charts are the same for top-down and toe-up versions.

Marama Left Foot Cable

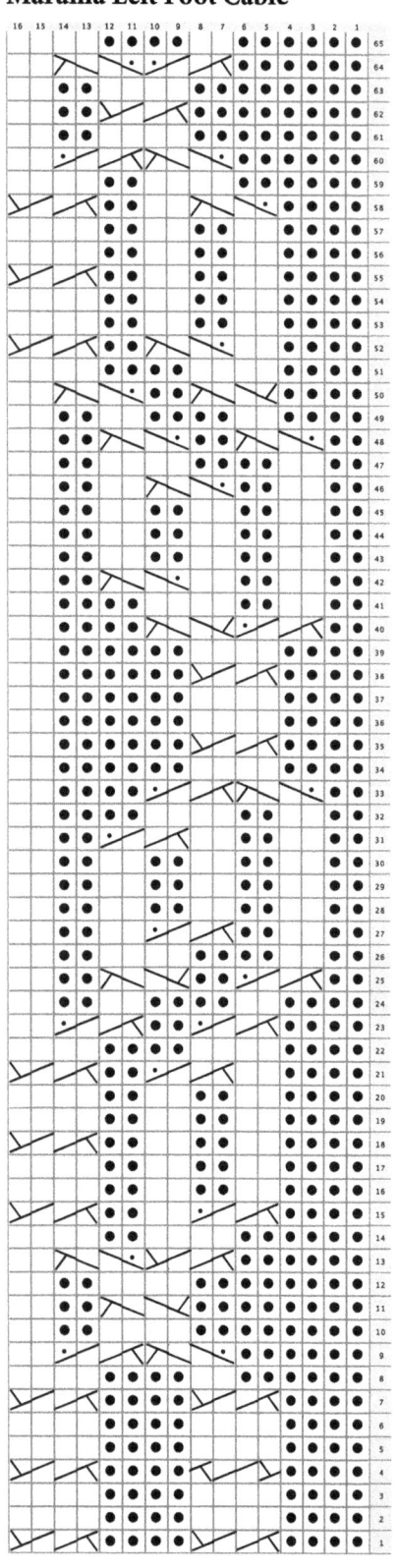

Marama Right Foot Cable

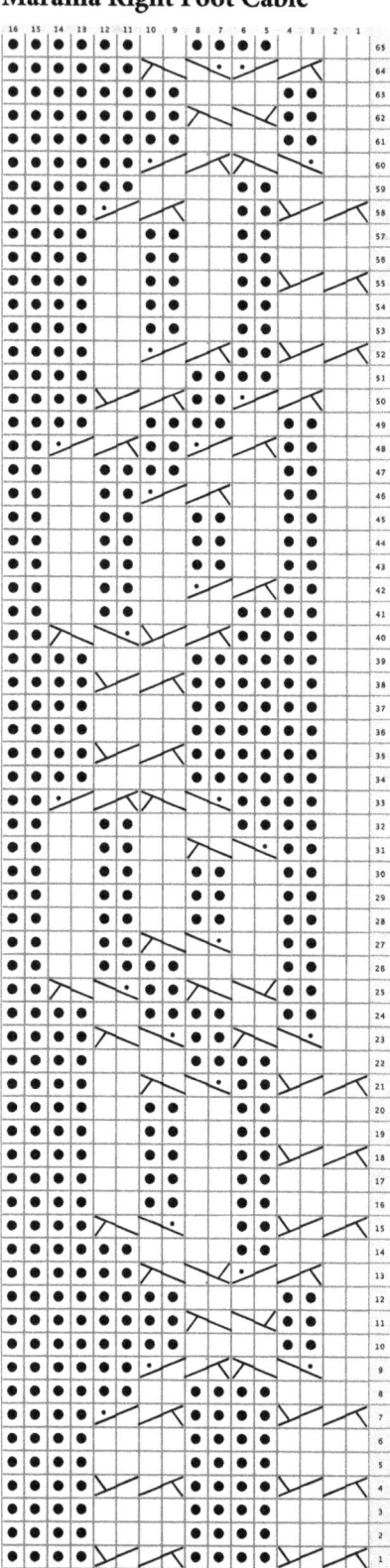

MARAMA TOP-DOWN WORKSHEET			
cast-on method	Choose your preferred cast-on method.		
circumference	10"	12"	14"
# of sts to cast on	66 sts	78 sts	90 sts
# of rnds per inch	10 rnds per inch		
placement of stitch patt	Start the 28 sts of the patt at the start of the rnd, using markers to separate this area from the rest of the sock. Complete all cuff rnds by working patt over the first 28 sts, then work: K1, [p2, k2] to last st, k1.		
length of cuff	3"	3"	3.5"
# of rnds in cuff	15 reps of Rnds 1 & 2, plus 1 rep of Rnd 3	15 reps of Rnds 1 & 2, plus 1 rep of Rnd 3	20 reps of Rnds 1 & 2, plus 1 rep of Rnd 3
# of sts in leg	66 sts	78 sts	90 sts
rnds in leg	Rnds 16–57		
# of sts for afterthought heel (50%)	33 sts	39 sts	45 sts
placement of stitch patt	Right foot: Rearrange sts so that the first 16 sts of the stitch patt are at the beg of your rnd, with a total of 33 (39, 45) sts for the front of your sock and the rem sts are at for the foot of your sock. Continue working patt as established over the 16 pattern sts at the beg of your rnd and in stockinette for the rest of the sts. Left foot: Rearrange sts so that there are 17 (23, 29) stockinette sts followed by the first 16 sts of the patt for the front of your sock and the rem 33 (39, 45) sts for the foot. Continue working patt by knitting the first 17 (23, 29) sts, working patt as established over 16 sts, and knitting all rem sts.		
length of foot minus toe	Use your own foot length, work Rnds 58–68, and then from Rnd 1 until you reach your desired length.		
toe type			
toe	Divide sts so you have 2 equal groups. If you have an odd number, add an extra decrease to one of the groups as you start your decrease pattern. Follow the toe pattern that best fits your toe in chapter 7.		
closure method	Join rem toe sts using kitchener stitch or 3-needle bind off.		
heel	Pick up heel sts and work the heel of your choice.		

MARAMA TOE-UP WORKSHEET			
cast-on method	Choose your preferred cast-on method.		
circumference	10"	12"	14"
# of rnds per inch	10 rnds per inch		
toe	Work a toe that ends with 66 sts.	Work a toe that ends with 78 sts.	Work a toe that ends with 90 sts.
foot pattern	Right foot: Arrange sts so that the first 16 sts of the stitch patt are at the beg of your rnd, with a total of 33 (39, 45) sts for the front of your sock and the rem sts are at the foot of your sock. Continue working patt as established over the 16 patt sts at the beg of your rnd and in stockinette for the rest of the sts. Left foot: Arrange sts so that there are 17 (23, 29) stockinette sts followed by the first 16 sts of the patt for the front of your sock and the rem 33 (39, 45) sts for the foot of your sock. Continue working patt by knitting the first 17 (23, 29) sts, working patt as established over 16 sts, and knitting all rem sts.		
foot length	Stitch patt needs to end on Rnd 57, For 6" of foot length, begin on Rnd 1, for every added inch, begin 10 rnds from end of patt.		
# of sts for afterthought heel	33 sts	39 sts	45 sts
leg length	Work from Rnd 58 to the end of the chart and then rep Rnds 1–16.		
leg pattern	Right foot: Work stitch patt over 12 sts before and current 16 sts (28 sts) and knit rem sts. Left foot: Work stitch patt over 16 existing and following 12 sts (28 sts) and knit rem sts.		
cuff length	3"	3"	3.5"
# of rnds in cuff	1 rep of Rnd 1, then 15 reps of Rnds 2 & 3	1 rep of Rnd 1, then 15 reps of Rnds 2 & 3	1 rep of Rnd 1, then 20 reps of Rnds 2 & 3
cuff pattern	Arrange sts so the 28th column of the stitch patt is at the beg of your rnd, pm just before and just after these 28 sts. Complete all cuff rnds by working patt over the first 28 sts, then work: K1, [p2, k2] to last st, k1.		
bind-off method	Work Jeny's Surprisingly Stretchy Bind Off.		
afterthought heel	Pick up heel sts and work the heel of your choice.		

Modifying the pattern

The Marama sock provides us with a great opportunity for changing things up. Even though the cable pattern is static in width, there are plenty of stockinette stitches around that cable that can hold increases and decreases. Just be sure to take the number of stitches into account when you're working out your numbers—it's going to be your total stitch count minus the 28 sts of the chart.

It's possible to add length to the top of the sock by just working rounds from the end of the pattern first. However, this is going to take some planning, and changing within the cuff.

For example, if you chose to work rounds 61–67 at the start of your sock, then your cuff is going to flow from round 61, and your cuff design could reflect those three 4-stitch cables in the center.

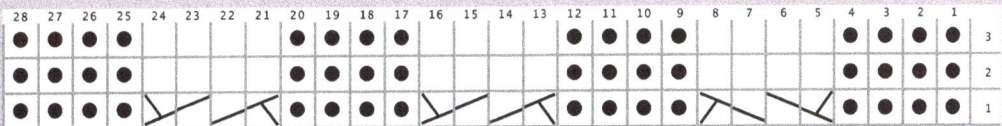

Wherever you choose to start your chart, be sure to take time beforehand to create a cuff that flows into your pattern, it's one of those design elements that really raises your sock from great to extraordinary!

Selu

Selu was the corn mother of the Cherokee nation. A goddess of the harvest who was revered for her wisdom, magic and hunting skills—how could I not name this sock after her? This pattern creates a very elastic fabric, with more grip and stretch. You may find that you need less shaping than in other socks to create the fit you desire.

MATERIALS

Shibui Sock (100% merino; 191 yds / 175m per 50g skein), 2 skeins; sample shown in Finch

US #1.5/2.5mm needles for working in the round: dpns, 2 short circulars or 1 longer circular

Cable needle (optional)
About 2 yds of waste cotton yarn in a similar weight

SIZE & FIT

Average foot circumference: 10.5 (13, 14.5)"
Sample shown in smallest size.

GAUGE

11 sts × 1.5 inches = one pattern repeat

Pattern repeat is 15 rnds high = 1.75", or 11 rnds per inch

Both versions: cuff

Work the following Cuff Rnd until cuff measures 3".

11	10	9	8	7	6	5	4	3	2	1
B	B	•	•	B	B	•	•	B	B	•

Both versions: leg & foot

11	10	9	8	7	6	5	4	3	2	1	
B	B	•	•	•	•	•	•	B	B	•	15
B	B	•	•	•	•	•	•	B	B	•	14
B	⋋	⋌	•	•	•	•	⋋	⋌	B	•	13
B	•	⋋	⋌	•	•	⋋	⋌	•	B	•	12
B	•	•	⋋	⋌	•	⋋	⋌	•	•	B	•	11
B	•	•	•	⋋	⋌	•	•	•	B	•	10
B	•	•	•	B	B	•	•	•	B	•	9
B	•	•	•	⋋	⋌	•	•	•	B	•	8
B	•	•	•	B	B	•	•	•	B	•	7
B	•	•	•	⋋	⋌	•	•	•	B	•	6
B	•	•	⋋	⋌	•	⋋	⋌	•	B	•	5
B	•	⋋	⋌	•	•	⋋	⋌	•	B	•	4
B	⋋	⋌	•	•	•	•	⋋	⋌	B	•	3
B	B	•	•	•	•	•	•	B	B	•	2
B	B	•	•	•	•	•	•	B	B	•	1

purl
purl stitch

knit tbl
Knit stitch through back loop

Left Twist, purl bg
sl1 to CN, hold in front. p1, k1 from CN

Right Twist, purl bg
sl1 to CN, hold in back. k1, p1 from CN

Left Twist
sl1 to CN, hold in front. k1, k1 from CN

SELU TOP-DOWN WORKSHEET			
cast-on method	Choose your preferred cast-on method.		
circumference	10.5"	13"	14.5"
# of sts to cast on	77 sts	88 sts	99 sts
# of rnds per inch	11 rnds per inch (patt repeat is 15 rnds)		
length of cuff	3"	3"	3"
# of rnds in cuff	33 rnds	33 rnds	33 rnds
leg length	Use your own leg length.		
# of rnds in leg	Work out your own # of rnds by multiplying leg length by 11 (number of rnds per inch)		
# of sts for afterthought heel	33 sts	44 sts	44 sts
foot pattern	Arrange sts so that you are starting at the beg of a patt rep and work 44 sts for front of sock; knit rem 33 sts with waste yarn, and then re-knit them with project yarn. Continue to work front of sock in patt and knit the 44 sts that make up the sole.	Arrange sts so that you have 4 complete patt reps for the front of your foot; knit rem 44 sts with waste yarn and then re-knit them with project yarn. Continue to work front of sock in patt and knit the 44 sts of the sole.	Work 5 reps of the patt as the front of your foot; knit rem 44 sts with waste yarn and then re-knit them with project yarn. Continue to work front of sock in patt and knit the sole.
length of foot minus toe	Use your own foot length.		
# of rnds in foot	Multiply foot length by rnds per inch (11).		
toe type			
toe	Divide sts so you have 2 equal groups. If you have an odd number, add an extra decrease to one of the groups as you start your decrease pattern. Follow the toe pattern that best fits your toe in chapter 7.		
closure method	Join rem toe sts using kitchener stitch or 3-needle bind off.		
heel	Pick up heel sts and work the heel of your choice.		

SELU TOE-UP WORKSHEET			
cast-on method	Choose your preferred cast-on method.		
circumference	10.5"	13"	14.5"
# of rnds per inch	11 rnds per inch		
toe	Work a toe that ends with 77 sts.	Work a toe that ends with 88 sts.	Work a toe that ends with 99 sts.
foot pattern	Arrange sts so you have 44 sts (4 reps) for the front of your sock, and 33 sts for the back. Work the first 44 sts in patt and the rem sts in stockinette.	Arrange sts so you have 44 sts (4 reps) for the front of your sock, and 44 sts for the back. Work the first 44 sts in patt and the rem sts in stockinette.	Arrange sts so you have 55 sts (5 reps) for the front of your sock, and 44 sts for the back. Work the first 55 sts in patt and the rem sts in stockinette.
foot length	Use your own foot length.		
# of rnds in foot	Work out your own # of rnds by multiplying foot length by 11 (number of rnds per inch).		
# of sts for afterthought heel	33 sts	44 sts	44 sts
leg length	Use your own leg length.		
# of rnds in leg	Leg length multiplied by rnd gauge (12).		
leg pattern	Work all sts in patt. End with Rnd 13, 14 or 15 for good flow into the cuff patt.		
cuff length	3 inches	3 inches	3 inches
length of cuff	3"	3"	3"
bind-off method	Work Jeny's Surprisingly Stretchy Bind Off.		
afterthought heel	Pick up heel sts and work the heel of your choice.		

Modifying the pattern

The heel numbers in this pattern were chosen by selecting a number that both was close to 50% of the total stitch count and allowed complete pattern repeats across the top of the foot.

While this pattern has a lot of ease, if you find you do need to make changes, consider either adding another column of purl stitches next to column 1 or deleting column 1 and 2 entirely.

Similarly, if you wish to incorporate shaping, it is best to add it before or after columns 1, 2 or 11.

Freya

Freya, the Norse goddess of love, beauty, wealth, fertility and war, was never one to be trifled with—and neither are her socks. The Northern Lights are said to be the result of Freya riding through the sky. This beautiful sock combines a twisted rib and eyelets to create a vertical pattern that you will love to knit and wear.

MATERIALS

1 skein Malabrigo Sock (100% merino wool; 440 yds / 402m per 100g skein), 2 skeins; sample shown in Lettuce

US #1.5/2.5mm needles for working in the round: dpns, 2 short circulars or 1 longer circular

About 2 yds of waste cotton yarn in a similar weight

SIZE & FIT

Average foot circumference: 10 (11.5, 13)" Sample shown in smallest size.

GAUGE

Pattern repeat (5 sts × 4 rnds) is ⅝" wide × ⅝" high after blocking.

PATTERN NOTES

If you wish to incorporate shaping, it is best to add it before columns 1, 2 and 3.

Both versions: cuff

Top-down version: leg & foot

Freya Top-Down Lace pattern

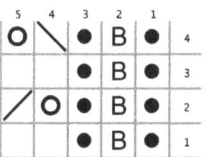

Toe-up version: leg & foot

Freya Toe-Up Lace pattern

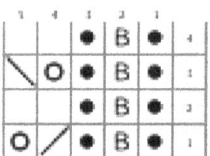

• **purl** — purl stitch		╱ **k2tog** — Knit two stitches together as one stitch
B **knit tbl** — Knit stitch through back loop		╲ **ssk** — Slip one stitch as if to knit, Slip another stitch as if to knit. Insert left-hand needle into front of these 2 stitches and knit them together
knit — knit stitch		
O **yo** — Yarn Over		

FREYA TOP-DOWN WORKSHEET			
cast-on method	Choose your preferred cast-on method.		
circumference	10"	11.5"	13"
# of sts to cast on	75 sts	90 sts	105 sts
# of rnds per inch	10 rnds per inch		
length of cuff	3"	3"	3.5"
# of rnds in cuff	30 rnds	30 rnds	35 rnds
leg length	Use your own leg length.		
# of rnds in leg	Work out your own # of rnds by multiplying leg length by 10 (number of rnds per inch).		
# of sts for afterthought heel	37 sts	42 sts	47 sts
note	*Front of sock stitch number calculated by using nearest multiple of 5 to 50% of sts plus 3-st column at beginning of pattern.*		
foot pattern	Work 38 sts in patt for front of sock; knit rem 37 sts with waste yarn, and then re-knit them with project yarn. Continue to work front of sock in patt and knit the 37 sts that make up the sole.	Work 48 sts in patt for front of sock; knit rem 42 sts with waste yarn, and then re-knit them with project yarn. Continue to work front of sock in patt and knit the 42 sts that make up the sole.	Work 58 sts in patt for front of sock; knit rem 47 sts with waste yarn, and then re-knit them with project yarn. Continue to work front of sock in patt and knit the 47 sts that make up the sole.
length of foot minus toe	Use your own foot length.		
# of rnds in foot	Multiply foot length by rnds per inch (10).		
toe type			
toe	Divide sts so you have 2 equal groups. If you have an odd number, add an extra decrease to one of the groups as you start your decrease pattern. Follow the toe pattern that best fits your toe in chapter 7.		
closure method	Join rem toe sts using kitchener stitch or 3-needle bind off.		
heel	Pick up heel sts and work the heel of your choice.		

FREYA TOE-UP WORKSHEET			
cast-on method	Choose your preferred cast-on method.		
circumference	10"	11.5"	13"
# of rnds per inch	10 rnds per inch		
toe	Work a toe that ends with 75 sts.	Work a toe that ends with 90 sts.	Work a toe that ends with 105 sts.
foot pattern	Work 38 sts in patt for front of sock and 37 sts in stockinette for sole.	Work 48 sts in patt for front of sock and 42 sts in stockinette for sole.	Work 58 sts in patt for front of sock and 47 sts in stockinette for sole.
foot length	Use your own foot length.		
# of rnds in foot	Work out your own # by multiplying foot length by 10 (rnds per inch).		
# of sts for afterthought heel	37 sts	42 sts	47 sts
afterthought heel	Knit sole sts with waste yarn, and then again with project yarn.		
leg length	Use your own leg length.		
# of rnds in leg	Leg length multiplied by rnd gauge (10).		
leg pattern	Work all rnds in patt.		
length of cuff	3"	3"	3.5"
# of rnds in cuff	30 rnds	30 rnds	35 rnds
bind-off method	Work Jeny's Surprisingly Stretchy Bind Off.		
afterthought heel	Pick up heel sts and work the heel of your choice.		

Modifying the pattern

Want to add shaping to the foot or leg of your sock? The first three columns of the stitch pattern don't change and so are a perfect place to add extra columns. Changing this first group of 3 sts from [p1, ktbl, p1] to [p2, ktbl, p2] will add 2 sts. Over a whole round, adding 2 sts to every repeat could amount to a very nice short increase. Another option is to add a new pattern repeat over a long increase section. One way to do this for a toe-up version is:

Rnd 1: P1, k tbl, p1, ssk, yo, p1, k tbl, p1.
Rnd 2: P1, k tbl, p1, k2, p1, (k yo k) in 1 st, p1.
Rnd 3: P1, k tbl, p1, yo, k2tog, p1, k tbl, p1, k tbl, p1.
Rnd 4: P1, k tbl, p1, k2, p1, k tbl, (k yo k) in 1 st, k tbl, p1.
Rnd 5: P1, k tbl, p1, ssk, yo, [p1, k tbl] 3 times, p1.
Rnd 6: P1, k tbl, p1, k2, [p1, k tbl] 3 times, p1.
Rnd 7: P1, k tbl, p1, yo, k2tog, p1, k tbl, p1, yo, k2tog, p1, m1R.
Rnd 8: P1, k tbl, p1, k2, p1, k tbl, p1, k2, p1, k tbl, p1.
Rnd 9: P1, k tbl, p1, ssk, yo, p1, k tbl, p1, ssk, yo, p1, k tbl, p1.
Rnd 10: P1, k tbl, p1, k2, p1, k tbl, p1, k2, p1, k tbl, p1.
Rnd 11: P1, k tbl, p1, yo, k2tog, p1, k tbl, p1, yo, k2tog, p1, k tbl, p1.
Rnd 12: P1, k tbl, p1, k2, p1, k tbl, p1, k2, p1, k tbl, p1.
Rnd 13: P1, k tbl, p1, ssk, yo, p1, k tbl, p1, ssk, yo, p1, k tbl, p1.
Rnd 14: P1, k tbl, p1, k2, p1, k tbl, p1, dbl dec, k tbl, p1.
Rnd 15: P1, k tbl, p1, yo, k2tog, p1, k tbl, p2, k tbl, p1.
Rnd 16: P1, k tbl, p1, k2, p1, k tbl, dbl dec, p1.
Rnd 17: P1, k tbl, p1, ssk, yo, p1, k tbl, p2.
Rnd 18: P1, k tbl, p1, k2, p1, k2tog, p1.
Rnd 19: P1, k tbl, p1, yo, k2tog, p1, k tbl, p1.
Rnd 20: P1, k tbl, p1, k2, p1, k tbl, p1.

Eos

Eos, the Greek goddess, woke every morning, donned a saffron robe, and used her rosy fingers to open the gates of Heaven. Just as the dawn begins the day, this is the perfect sock for a beginner to step into their sock knitting adventure. With simple cables and an easy-to-remember pattern, you'll still enjoy enough variety to keep your knitting interesting.

MATERIALS

MadelineTosh Tosh Sock (100% superwash merino; 395 yds / 361m per 114g skein), 1 skein; sample shown in Tomato

US #1.5/2.5mm needles for working in the round: dpns, 2 short circulars or 1 longer circular

Cable needle
About 2 yds of waste cotton yarn in a similar weight

SIZE & FIT

Average foot circumference: 10 (11.5, 13)"
Sample shown in smallest size.

GAUGE

Pattern repeat (14 sts × 17 rnds) = 1.75" wide × 1.5" high

PATTERN NOTES

With lots of uninterrupted columns of stitches in this pattern, there are plenty of opportunities to add stitches in either long or short increases and similarly so with decreases.

Top-down version

See page 85 for chart key.

Cuff Pattern

Body Pattern

EOS TOP-DOWN WORKSHEET			
cast-on method	Choose your preferred cast-on method.		
circumference	10"	11.5"	13"
# of sts to cast on	114 sts	133 sts	152 sts
# of rnds per inch	12 rnds per inch		
length of cuff	3"	3"	3"
cuff pattern	Work Rnds 1–3 of cuff patt for 2.5", then rem rnds once.		
# of sts in leg	84 sts	98 sts	112 sts
leg length	Use your own leg length.		
# of rnds in leg	Work out your own # of rnds by multiplying leg length by 12 (number of rnds per inch).		
# of sts for afterthought heel	37 sts	37 sts	51 sts
foot pattern	Work 47 sts in patt (3 reps plus 5 sts) for front of sock; knit rem 37 sts with waste yarn, and then re-knit them with project yarn. Continue to work front of sock in patt and knit the 37 sts that make up the sole.	Work 61 sts in patt (4 reps plus 5 sts) for front of sock; knit rem 37 sts with waste yarn, and then re-knit them with project yarn. Continue to work front of sock in patt and knit the 37 sts that make up the sole.	Work 61 sts in patt (4 reps plus 5 sts) for front of sock; knit rem 51 sts with waste yarn, and then re-knit them with project yarn. Continue to work front of sock in patt and knit the 51 sts that make up the sole.
length of foot minus toe	Use your own foot length.		
# of rnds in foot	Multiply foot length by rnds per inch (12).		
toe type			
toe	Divide sts so you have 2 equal groups. If you have an odd number, add an extra decrease to one of the groups as you start your decrease pattern. Follow the toe pattern that best fits your toe in chapter 7.		
closure method	Join rem toe sts using kitchener stitch or 3-needle bind off.		
heel	Pick up heel sts and work the heel of your choice.		

EOS TOE-UP WORKSHEET			
cast-on method	Choose your preferred cast-on method.		
circumference	10"	11.5"	13"
# of rnds per inch	12 rnds per inch		
toe	Work a toe that ends with 84 sts.	Work a toe that ends with 98 sts.	Work a toe that ends with 112 sts.
foot pattern	Arrange sts so the last 2 sts of bottom of foot move to top of foot for patt. Work 47 sts in patt for front of foot (3 reps plus 5 sts) and 37 sts in stockinette for sole.	Arrange sts so the last 2 sts of bottom of foot move to top of foot for patt. Work 61 sts in patt for front of foot (4 reps plus 5 sts) and 37 sts in stockinette for sole.	Arrange sts so the last 2 sts of bottom of foot move to top of foot for patt. Work 61 sts in patt for front of foot (4 reps plus 5 sts) and 51 sts in stockinette for sole.
foot length	Use your own foot length.		
# of rnds in foot	Work out your own # of rnds by multiplying foot length by 12 (number of rnds per inch).		
# of sts for afterthought heel	37 sts	37 sts	51 sts
afterthought heel	Knit the heel sts in waste yarn and then again in project yarn.		
leg length	Use your own leg length.		
# of rnds in leg	Leg length multiplied by rnd gauge (12).		
leg pattern	Work all sts in patt, keeping continuity of patt on front of foot.		
cuff length	3"	3"	3"
cuff	Work Rnds 1–3 once, then rep Rnds 4–6 until cuff measures 3".		
bind-off method	Work Jeny's Surprisingly Stretchy Bind Off.		
afterthought heel	Pick up heel sts and work the heel of your choice.		

Toe-up version

Body Pattern

Cuff Pattern

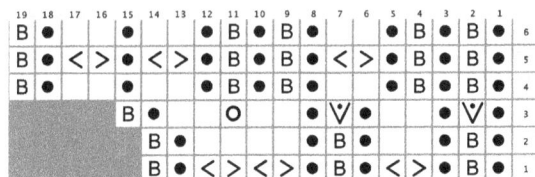

•	**purl** purl stitch	
B	**knit tbl** Knit stitch through back loop	
<|>	**two stitch wrap** with yarn in back, slip next 2 sts from LHN to RHN, with yarn in front, slip same 2 sts back to LHN, knit the 2 sts.	
▓	**No Stitch** Placeholder – No stitch made.	
☐	**knit** knit stitch	
V	**(k1 p1 k1) in 1 st** knit, purl and knit again all in the same st to make 3 sts from 1	
O	**yo** Yarn Over	
╱╲	**c2 over 1 right P** sl1 to CN, hold in back. k2, p1 from CN	
╲╱	**c2 over 1 left P** sl2 to CN, hold in front. p1, k2 from CN	
╲╱╲	**c2 over 2 right** sl2 to CN, hold in back. k2, k2 from CN	

Alcyone

On hearing of her husband's death, Alcyone threw herself into the sea and drowned. However, the Greek gods took pity on her and turned her into a kingfisher. This pretty kingfisher blue sock is perfect for variegated yarn. Wrapped stitches and stitches knit through the back loop create a tight-fitting sock that's ideal for long increases and decreases.

MATERIALS

Three Irish Girls Beckon Merino (100% merino; 370 yds / 338m per 100g skein), 1 skein; sample uses "Zephyr"

US #1.5/2.5mm needles for working in the round: dpns, 2 short circulars or 1 longer circular

About 2 yds of waste cotton yarn in a similar weight

SIZE & FIT

Average foot circumference: 10 (12, 14)"
Sample shown in smallest size.

GAUGE

Pattern repeat (16 sts × 23 rnds) = 2" square

PATTERN NOTES

Because the whole sock is worked in what is basically a rib, the cuff is only 2" high.

Column 1 is the only column of stitches that does not change throughout the pattern. Long increases or short increases can be placed here without changing the stitch pattern.

Top-down version

16	15	14	13	12	11	10	9	8	7	6	5	4	3	2	1	
<	O	>	●	B	●	B	●	B	●	B	●	<	O	>	●	23
B	●	B	●	B	●	B	●	B	●	B	●	B	●	B	●	22
B	●	<	O	>	●	B	●	B	●	<	O	>	●	B	●	21
B	●	B	●	B	●	B	●	B	●	B	●	B	●	B	●	20
<	O	>	●	<	O	>	●	<	O	>	●	<	O	>	●	19
B	●	B	●	B	●	B	●	B	●	B	●	B	●	B	●	18
B	●	<	O	>	●	<	O	>	●	<	O	>	●	B	●	17
B	●	B	●	B	●	B	●	B	●	B	●	B	●	B	●	16
<	O	>	●	<	O	>	●	<	O	>	●	<	O	>	●	15
B	●	B	●	B	●	B	●	B	●	B	●	B	●	B	●	14
B	●	<	O	>	●	<	O	>	●	<	O	>	●	B	●	13
B	●	B	●	B	●	B	●	B	●	B	●	B	●	B	●	12
B	●	B	●	<	O	>	●	<	O	>	●	B	●	B	●	11
B	●	B	●	B	●	B	●	B	●	B	●	B	●	B	●	10
B	●	B	●	B	●	<	O	>	●	B	●	B	●	B	●	9
B	●	B	●	B	●	B	●	B	●	B	●	B	●	B	●	8
B	●	B	●	B	●	B	●	B	●	B	●	B	●	B	●	7
B	●	B	●	B	●	B	●	B	●	B	●	B	●	B	●	6
B	●	B	●	B	●	B	●	B	●	B	●	B	●	B	●	5
B	●	B	●	B	●	B	●	B	●	B	●	B	●	B	●	4
B	●	B	●	B	●	B	●	B	●	B	●	B	●	B	●	3
B	●	B	●	B	●	B	●	B	●	B	●	B	●	B	●	2
B	●	B	●	B	●	B	●	B	●	B	●	B	●	B	●	1

● purl
purl stitch

<O> 3 st yo wrap
with yib, slip next 3 sts onto rh needle, with yif, slip back, k1, yo, k2tog.

B knit tbl
Knit stitch through back loop

ALCYONE TOP-DOWN WORKSHEET			
cast-on method	Choose your preferred cast-on method.		
circumference	10"	12"	14"
# of sts to cast on	80 sts	96 sts	112 sts
# of rnds per inch	12 rnds per inch		
length of cuff	2"	2"	2"
# of rnds in cuff	24 rnds	24 rnds	24 rnds
cuff patt	Work Rnd 1 a total of 24 times.		
# of sts in leg	80 sts	96 sts	112 sts
leg length	Use your own leg length.		
# of rnds in leg	Work out your own # of rnds by multiplying leg length by 12 (number of rnds per inch).		
# of sts for afterthought heel	40 sts	48 sts	56 sts
foot pattern	Work 40 sts in patt for front of sock; knit rem 40 sts with waste yarn, and then re-knit them with project yarn. Continue to work front of sock in patt and knit the 40 sts that make up the sole.	Work 48 sts in patt for front of sock; knit rem 48 sts with waste yarn, and then re-knit them with project yarn. Continue to work front of sock in patt and knit the 48 sts that make up the sole.	Work 56 sts in patt for front of sock; knit rem 56 sts with waste yarn, and then re-knit them with project yarn. Continue to work front of sock in patt and knit the 56 sts that make up the sole.
length of foot minus toe	Use your own foot length.		
# of rnds in foot	Multiply foot length by rnds per inch (12).		
toe type			
toe	Divide sts so you have 2 equal groups. If you have an odd number, add an extra decrease to one of the groups as you start your decrease pattern. Follow the toe pattern that best fits your toe in chapter 7.		
closure method	Join rem toe sts using kitchener stitch or 3-needle bind off.		
heel	Pick up heel sts and work the heel of your choice.		

Toe-up version

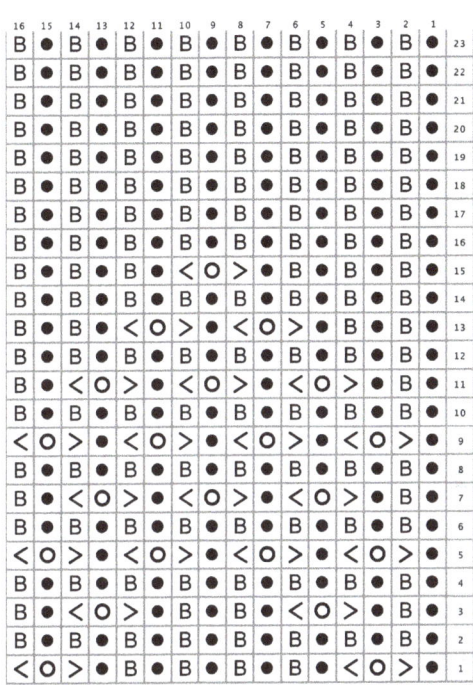

- ● **purl** — purl stitch
- <○> **3 st yo wrap** — with yib, slip next 3 sts onto rh needle, with yif, slip back, k1, yo, k2tog.
- B **knit tbl** — Knit stitch through back loop

ALCYONE TOE-UP WORKSHEET			
cast-on method	Choose your preferred cast-on method.		
circumference	10"	12"	14"
# of rnds per inch	12 rnds per inch		
toe	Work a toe that ends with 80 sts.	Work a toe that ends with 96 sts.	Work a toe that ends with 112 sts.
foot pattern	Work front of sock in patt and back of sock in stockinette.		
foot length	Use your own foot length.		
# of rnds in foot	Work out your own # of rnds by multiplying foot length by 12 (number of rnds per inch).		
# of sts for afterthought heel	40 sts	48 sts	66 sts
afterthought heel	Work front of sock in patt; knit heel sts with waste yarn; then re-knit heel sts using project yarn.		
leg length	Use your own leg length.		
# of rnds in leg	Leg length multiplied by rnd gauge (12).		
leg pattern	Work all sts in patt, keeping continuity of patt rnds as established.		
cuff length	2"	2"	2"
cuff pattern	Work 24 Cuff Rnds (3 repeats of Rnds 16–23 above).		
cuff	Rep Rnd 23 of stitch patt 24 more times for cuff.		
bind-off method	Work Jeny's Surprisingly Stretchy Bind Off.		
afterthought heel	Pick up heel sts and work the heel of your choice.		

Modifying the pattern

Out of the 16 columns in the Alcyone chart, 15 create the heart of the stitch pattern. To alter the number of stitches in this sock, then, you should make changes around the very first purl column. You may choose to put an extra [k1tbl, p1] doublet in each repeat, for example, or work a long increase along the column.

Let's look at some examples. Here are the original stitch counts and pattern repeats for these socks:

# of sts in original sock	# of pattern repeats
80	5
96	6
112	7

Suppose we decide to add an extra [k1tbl, p1] before each pattern repeat. Here's what would result:

# of sts increased	new # of sts in sock
5 × 2 = 10	90
6 × 2 = 12	108
7 × 2 = 14	126

Alternatively, we could increase 1 purl stitch on 2 (3, 3) pattern repeats every 5th round 5 (6, 7) times, which would give us:

# of sts increased	new # of sts in sock
2 × 5 = 10	90
3 × 6 = 18	114
3 × 7 = 21	133

Arundhati

Arundhati is the Hindu goddess associated with the morning star. The gradation in this yarn goes from purple to orange and reminds me very much of a sunrise in this charming sock. A delicate ribbed pattern is the perfect foil to let the yarn be the superstar of this sock.

MATERIALS

Unique Sheep Luxe (75% superwash merino, 25% tussah silk; 400 yds per 100g set), 1 set of 6 mini-skeins; sample shown in Daybreak

US #1.5/2.5mm needles for working in the round: dpns, 2 short circulars or 1 longer circular

About 2 yds of waste cotton yarn in a similar weight

SIZE & FIT

Average foot circumference: 10 (11.5, 13)" Sample shown in smallest size.

GAUGE

Pattern repeat (10 sts × 4 rnds) = 1.5" wide × 0.33" high.

PATTERN NOTES

For tips on working with Gradiance yarns, visit www.theuniquesheep.com/tutorials/gradiancesocks/

For top-down socks, begin knitting with the first color. Change colors about halfway down the leg, again right before heel flap, and again at about halfway through the foot. For toe-up socks, simply reverse the process.

When changing colors, change from one ball to the next gradually. Otherwise you will create stripes. For a gradual color change, alternate as follows: 2 rnds new color; 4 rnds old color; 4 rnds new color; 2 rnds old color.

In between color changes, work all rounds with one color. If you run out of one of the yarns while changing colors it's OK, as long as you've had a chance to complete some of the alternating rows.

For top-down socks, work skeins 1–6 in numerical order; for toe-up, work the skeins in reverse order from 6 to 1 so the lighter color is at the cuff and the darker color is at the toe.

If you want continuity of color throughout your whole sock, be sure to keep enough yarn from the skein you're using at the afterthought heel round to work the heel.

Both versions: stitch patterns

Cuff pattern
Cuff Rnd: [P1, k1] around.

Leg and foot pattern
Pattern worked the same top down and toe up.

- ● **purl** — purl stitch
- ○ **yo** — Yarn Over
- □ **knit** — knit stitch
- ⋏ **Central Double Dec** — Slip first and second stitches together as if to knit. Knit 1 stitch. Pass two slipped stitches over the knit stitch.

ARUNDHATI TOP-DOWN WORKSHEET			
cast-on method	Choose your preferred cast-on method.		
circumference	10"	11.5"	13"
# of sts to cast on	70 sts	80 sts	90 sts
# of rnds per inch	12 rnds per inch		
length of cuff	3"	3"	3"
# of rnds in cuff	36 rnds	36 rnds	36 rnds
# of sts in leg	70 sts	80 sts	90 sts
leg length	Use your own leg length.		
# of rnds in leg	Work out your own # of rnds by multiplying leg length by 12 (number of rnds per inch).		
# of sts for afterthought heel	34 sts	39 sts	44 sts
foot pattern	Work 36 sts in patt for front of sock; knit rem 34 sts with waste yarn, and then re-knit them with project yarn. Continue to work front of sock in patt and sole sts in stockinette.	Work 41 sts in patt for front of sock; knit rem 39 sts with waste yarn, and then re-knit them with project yarn. Continue to work front of sock in patt and sole sts in stockinette.	Work 46 sts in patt for front of sock; knit rem 44 sts with waste yarn, and then re-knit them with project yarn. Continue to work front of sock in patt and sole sts in stockinette.
length of foot minus toe	Use your own foot length.		
# of rnds in foot	Multiply foot length by rnds per inch (12).		
toe type			
toe	Divide sts so you have 2 equal groups. If you have an odd number, add an extra decrease to one of the groups as you start your decrease pattern. Follow the toe pattern that best fits your toe in chapter 7.		
closure method	Join rem toe sts using kitchener stitch or 3-needle bind off.		
heel	Pick up heel sts and work the heel of your choice.		

ARUNDHATI TOE-UP WORKSHEET			
cast-on method	Choose your preferred cast-on method.		
circumference	10"	11.5"	13"
# of rnds per inch	12 rnds per inch		
toe	Work a toe that ends with 70 sts.	Work a toe that ends with 80 sts.	Work a toe that ends with 90 sts.
foot pattern	Work 36 sts in patt for front of foot; rem 34 sts in stockinette for sole.	Work 41 sts in patt for front of foot; rem 39 sts in stockinette for sole.	Work 46 sts in patt for front of foot; rem 44 sts in stockinette for sole.
foot length	Use your own foot length.		
# of rnds in foot	Work out your own # of rnds by multiplying foot length by 12 (number of rnds per inch).		
# of sts for afterthought heel	34 sts	39 sts	44 sts
afterthought heel rnd	Work front section of sts in patt as established. Work sts for afterthought heel by knitting them once with waste yarn, and again with project yarn.		
leg length	Use your own leg length.		
# of rnds in leg	Leg length multiplied by rnd gauge (12).		
leg pattern	Work all sts in patt as established, keeping continuity as set.		
cuff length	3"	3"	3"
cuff pattern	Work 36 Cuff Rnds.		
bind-off method	Work Jeny's Surprisingly Stretchy Bind Off.		
afterthought heel	Pick up heel sts and work the heel of your choice.		

Modifying the pattern

Finding a way to alter stitch count while still keeping the integrity of the ribbed columns is key for this pattern. Depending on how many stitches you need to increase, you could either work a kfb in columns 2, 8 and 10, or work a pfb in columns 1, 3, 7 and 9 (or any combination thereof). Here are two examples of how that would work:

# of sts in original sock	# of pattern repeats
70	7
80	8
90	9

If we try the first increase method—adding a kfb to columns 2, 8, and 10—here's how the stitch count changes:

# of sts increased	new # of sts in sock
3 × 7 = 21	70 + 21 = 91
3 × 8 = 24	80 + 24 = 104
3 × 9 = 27	90 + 27 = 117

Instead, what if we decide to add a pfb to columns 1, 3, 5, and 7?

# of sts increased	new # of sts in sock
4 × 7 = 28	70 + 28 = 98
4 × 8 = 32	80 + 32 = 112
4 × 9 = 36	90 + 36 = 126

Mielikki

The Finnish goddess of the forest and the hunt, Mielikki tends to wounded animals, especially those who have been trapped. The verdant hues of this yarn bring to mind walks through the old-growth forests that I played in growing up in Yorkshire. These socks would have been perfect for keeping my feet warm on cold, muddy autumn days.

MATERIALS

Yarn Love Marianne Dashwood (100% superwash merino wool; 330 yds / 302m per 115g skein), 1 skein; sample shown in Lagoon colorway

US #1.5/2.5mm needles for working in the round: dpns, 2 short circulars or 1 longer circular

Cable needle
About 2 yds of waste cotton yarn in a similar weight

SIZE & FIT

Average foot circumference: 10 (12.5, 15)"
Sample shown in smallest size.

GAUGE

Pattern repeat (10 sts × 14 rnds) = 1.25" wide × 1.125" high

Both versions: stitch patterns

Leg and foot pattern

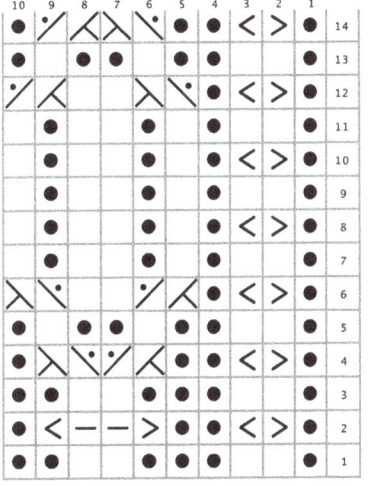

knit
knit stitch

purl
purl stitch

Left Twist, purl bg
sl1 to CN, hold in front. p1. k1 from CN

Right Twist, purl bg
sl1 to CN, hold in back. k1, p1 from CN

4 st wrap
With yarn in back, slip next 4 sts, bring yarn forward, slip 4 sts back to LH needle, wrap 2 more times, then k1b, p2, k1b,

two stitch wrap
with yarn in back, slip next 2 sts from LHN to RHN, with yarn in front, slip same 2 sts back to LHN, knit the 2 sts.

Cuff pattern

MIELIKKI TOP-DOWN WORKSHEET			
cast-on method	Choose your preferred cast-on method.		
circumference	10"	12.5"	15"
# of sts to cast on	80 sts	100 sts	120 sts
# of rnds per inch	12 rnds per inch		
length of cuff	3"	3"	3"
# of rnds in cuff	36 rnds	36 rnds	36 rnds
# of sts in leg	80 sts	100 sts	120 sts
leg length	Use your own leg length.		
# of rnds in leg	Work out your own # of rnds by multiplying leg length by 12 (number of rnds per inch).		
# of sts for afterthought heel	36 sts	46 sts	56 sts
foot pattern	Work 44 sts in patt for front of sock (4 reps plus 4 sts); knit rem 36 sts with waste yarn, and then re-knit them with project yarn. Continue to work front of sock in patt and sole sts in stockinette.	Work 54 sts in patt for front of sock (5 reps plus 4 sts); knit rem 46 sts with waste yarn, and then re-knit them with project yarn. Continue to work front of sock in patt and sole sts in stockinette.	Work 64 sts in patt for front of sock (6 reps plus 4 sts); knit rem 56 sts with waste yarn, and then re-knit them with project yarn. Continue to work front of sock in patt and sole sts in stockinette.
length of foot minus toe	Use your own foot length.		
# of rnds in foot	Multiply foot length by rnds per inch (12).		
toe	Divide sts so you have 2 equal groups. If you have an odd number, add an extra decrease to one of the groups as you start your decrease pattern. Follow the toe pattern that best fits your toe in chapter 7.		
closure method	Join rem toe sts using kitchener stitch or 3-needle bind off.		
heel	Pick up heel sts and work the heel of your choice.		

MIELIKKI TOE-UP WORKSHEET			
cast-on method	Choose your preferred cast-on method.		
circumference	10"	12.5"	15"
# of rnds per inch	12 rnds per inch		
toe	Work a toe that ends with 80 sts.	Work a toe that ends with 100 sts.	Work a toe that ends with 120 sts.
foot pattern	Arrange sts so you are working with 44 sts for front of sock and 36 sts for sole. Work first section in patt and second section in stockinette.	Arrange sts so you are working with 54 sts for front of sock and 46 sts for sole. Work first section in patt and second section in stockinette.	Arrange sts so you are working with 64 sts for front of sock and 56 sts for sole. Work first section in patt and second section in stockinette.
foot length	Use your own foot length.		
# of rnds in foot	Work out your own # of rnds by multiplying foot length by 12 (number of rnds per inch).		
# of sts for afterthought heel	36 sts	46 sts	56 sts
afterthought heel rnd	Work front section of sts in patt as established. Work sts for afterthought heel by knitting them once with waste yarn, and again with project yarn.		
leg length	Use your own leg length.		
# of rnds in leg	Leg length multiplied by rnd gauge (12).		
leg pattern	Work all sts in patt as established.		
cuff length	3"	3"	3"
cuff pattern	Work 36 Cuff Rnds.		
bind-off method	Work Jeny's Surprisingly Stretchy Bind Off.		
afterthought heel	Pick up heel sts and work the heel of your choice.		

Modifying the pattern

Whether you choose to work a long increase along the third pattern repeat of unchanging columns 1 and 4, or you choose to work short increases along all the repeats, or perhaps even add a repeat of columns 1–4 to the third and sixth pattern repeat, modifying this sock is simpler than the involved pattern first appears.

Depending on the number of stitches you need to alter your pattern by, you could even choose to add an extra triplet of columns 1–4 that run up either side of your leg!

Sionnan

Sionnan was the goddess of the River Shannon and queen of the water sprites in Ireland. This pattern is so named for Shannon Okey, founder of Cooperative Press and my friend.

MATERIALS

String Theory Colorworks Continuum (100% Bluefaced Leicester wool; 400 yds per 100g skein), 1 skein; sample shown in Stardust

US #1.5/2.5mm needles for working in the round: dpns, 2 short circulars or 1 longer circular

About 2 yds of waste cotton yarn in a similar weight

SIZE & FIT

Average foot circumference: 10 (11.25, 12.5)" Sample shown in smallest size.

GAUGE

Pattern repeat (10 sts × 12 rnds) = 1.5" square

Both versions: cuff

Cuff Rnd: [P1, k tbl] around.

Top-down version: leg & foot

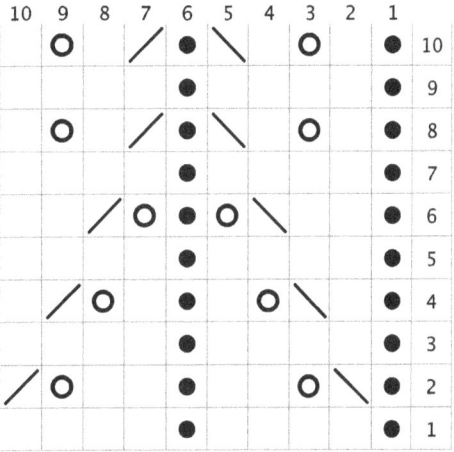

Toe-up version: leg & foot

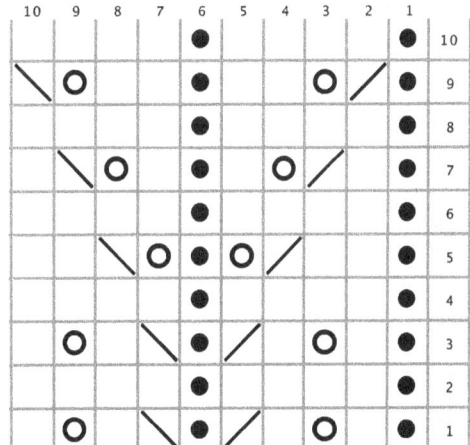

- **purl** — purl stitch
- **knit** — knit stitch
- **yo** — Yarn Over
- **k2tog** — Knit two stitches together as one stitch
- **ssk** — Slip one stitch as if to knit, Slip another stitch as if to knit. Insert left-hand needle into front of these 2 stitches and knit them together

SIONNAN TOP-DOWN WORKSHEET			
cast-on method	Choose your preferred cast-on method.		
circumference	10"	11.25"	12.5"
# of sts to cast on	80 sts	90 sts	100 sts
# of rnds per inch	12 rnds per inch		
length of cuff	3"	3"	3.5"
cuff pattern	Work 36 repeats of cuff patt.		
# of sts in leg	80 sts	90 sts	100 sts
leg length	Use your own leg length.		
# of rnds in leg	Work out your own # of rnds by multiplying leg length by 12 (number of rnds per inch).		
# of sts for afterthought heel	39 sts	44 sts	49 sts
foot pattern	Work 41 sts in patt for front of sock; knit rem 39 sts with waste yarn, and then re-knit them with project yarn. Continue to work front of sock in patt and sole sts in stockinette.	Work 46 sts in patt for front of sock; knit rem 44 sts with waste yarn, and then re-knit them with project yarn. Continue to work front of sock in patt and sole sts in stockinette.	Work 51 sts in patt for front of sock; knit rem 49 sts with waste yarn, and then re-knit them with project yarn. Continue to work front of sock in patt and sole sts in stockinette.
length of foot minus toe	Use your own foot length.		
# of rnds in foot	Multiply foot length by rnds per inch (12).		
toe type			
toe	Divide sts so you have 2 equal groups. If you have an odd number, add an extra decrease to one of the groups as you start your decrease pattern. Follow the toe pattern that best fits your toe in chapter 7.		
closure method	Join rem toe sts using kitchener stitch or 3-needle bind off.		
heel	Pick up heel sts and work the heel of your choice.		

SIONNAN TOE-UP WORKSHEET			
cast-on method	Choose your preferred cast-on method.		
circumference	10"	11.25"	12.5"
# of rnds per inch	12 rnds per inch		
toe	Work a toe that ends with 80 sts.	Work a toe that ends with 90 sts.	Work a toe that ends with 100 sts.
foot pattern	Work 41 sts in patt (4 reps plus 1) and rem 39 sts in stockinette.	Work 46 sts in patt (4 reps plus 6) and rem 44 sts in stockinette.	Work 51 sts in patt (5 reps plus 1) and rem 49 sts in stockinette.
foot length	Use your own foot length.		
# of rnds in foot	Work out your own # of rnds by multiplying foot length by 12 (number of rnds per inch).		
# of sts for afterthought heel	39 sts	44 sts	49 sts
afterthought heel rnd	Work front section of sts in patt as established. Work sts for afterthought heel by knitting them once with waste yarn, and again with project yarn.		
leg length	Use your own leg length.		
# of rnds in leg	Leg length multiplied by rnd gauge (12).		
leg pattern	Work all sts in patt as established.		
cuff length	3"	3"	3.5"
cuff pattern	Work 36 Cuff Rnds.		
bind-off method	Work Jeny's Surprisingly Stretchy Bind Off.		
afterthought heel	Pick up heel sts and work the heel of your choice.		

Modifying the pattern

In this design, purl columns 1 and 6 are the places to add stitches. If you have an increase that remains permanent, try changing one of these two purl columns into a [p1, k1, p1] triplet instead. This will change the overall look of the pattern, but will enhance rather than take away the inherent style.

If we change the column 1 purl stitch to a [p1, k1, p1] triplet, here's what happens:

# of sts in original sock	# of pattern repeats	# of sts increased	new # of sts in sock
80	8	8 × 2 = 16	80 + 16 = 96
90	9	9 × 2 = 18	90 + 18 = 108
100	10	10 × 2 = 20	100 + 20 = 120

Eidothea

Daughter of the Greek sea god Proteus, the nymph Eidothea was known for her knowledge and womanly curves. The multiple yarnovers in the lace create a flowing fabric with lots of room. Like the ocean, these socks will hug onto your skin comfortably without constraining or binding you.

MATERIALS

Spud & Chloë Fine (80% wool/20% silk; 248 yds/227m per 65g skein), 2 skeins; sample shown in Calypso # 7806

US #1.5/2.5mm needles for working in the round: dpns, 2 short circulars or 1 longer circular

Cable needle
About 4 yds of waste cotton yarn in a similar weight

SIZE & FIT

Average foot circumference: 10.5 (12.25, 14)"
Sample shown in smallest size.

GAUGE

Pattern repeat (10 sts × 10 rnds) = 1.75" wide × 1.5" high

Both versions: cuff

Rnds 1–6: Knit.
Rnd 7: [K2tog, yo] around.
Rnds 8–13: Knit.

Top-down version: leg & foot

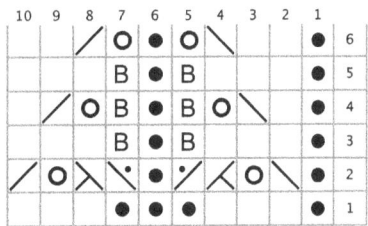

Toe-up version: leg & foot

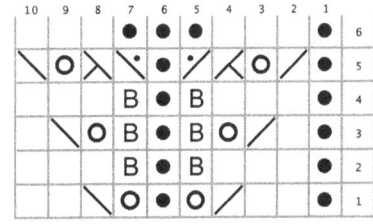

- **purl** — purl stitch
- **knit** — knit stitch
- **ssk** — Slip one stitch as if to knit, Slip another stitch as if to knit. Insert left-hand needle into front of these 2 stitches and knit them together
- **yo** — Yarn Over
- **Right Twist, purl bg** — sl1 to CN, hold in back. k1, p1 from CN
- **Left Twist, purl bg** — sl1 to CN, hold in front. p1, k1 from CN
- **k2tog** — Knit two stitches together as one stitch
- **knit tbl** — Knit stitch through back loop

EIDOTHEA TOP-DOWN WORKSHEET			
cast-on method	Choose your preferred cast-on method.		
circumference	10.5"	12.25"	14"
# of sts to cast on	60 sts	70 sts	80 sts
cuff	Work Rnds 1–13 of cuff.		
# of sts in leg	60 sts	70 sts	80 sts
leg length	Use your own leg length.		
# of rnds in leg	Work out your own # of rnds by multiplying leg length by 7.5 (number of rnds per inch).		
# of sts for afterthought heel	29 sts	34 sts	39 sts
foot pattern	Work 31 sts in patt for front of sock (3 reps plus 1); knit rem 29 sts with waste yarn, and then re-knit them with project yarn. Continue to work front of sock in patt and sole sts in stockinette.	Work 36 sts in patt for front of sock (3 reps plus 6); knit rem 34 sts with waste yarn, and then re-knit them with project yarn. Continue to work front of sock in patt and sole sts in stockinette.	Work 41 sts in patt for front of sock (4 reps plus 1); knit rem 39 sts with waste yarn, and then re-knit them with project yarn. Continue to work front of sock in patt and sole sts in stockinette.
length of foot minus toe	Use your own foot length.		
# of rnds in foot	Multiply foot length by rnds per inch (7.5).		
toe type			
toe	Divide sts so you have 2 equal groups. If you have an odd number, add an extra decrease to one of the groups as you start your decrease pattern. Follow the toe pattern that best fits your toe in chapter 7.		
closure method	Join rem toe sts using kitchener stitch or 3-needle bind off.		
heel	Pick up heel sts and work the heel of your choice.		
finishing	Once your sock is finished, fold down the cuff at the yo rnd and loosely sew the first rnd to the last rnd on the inside.		

EIDOTHEA TOE-UP WORKSHEET			
cast-on method	Choose your preferred cast-on method.		
circumference	10.5"	12.25"	14"
# of rnds per inch	7.5 rnds per inch		
toe	Work a toe that ends with 60 sts.	Work a toe that ends with 70 sts.	Work a toe that ends with 80 sts.
foot pattern	Work 31 sts in patt (3 reps plus 1 st) and rem 29 sts in stockinette.	Work 36 sts in patt (3 reps plus 6 sts) and rem 34 sts in stockinette.	Work 41 sts in patt (4 reps plus 1 st) and rem 39 sts in stockinette.
foot length	Use your own foot length.		
# of rnds in foot	Work out your own # of rnds by multiplying foot length by 7.5 (number of rnds per inch).		
# of sts for afterthought heel	31 sts	36 sts	39 sts
leg length	Use your own leg length.		
# of rnds in leg	Leg length multiplied by rnd gauge (7.5).		
leg pattern	Work all sts in patt as established.		
cuff	Work Rnds 1–13 of cuff.		
bind-off method	Work Jeny's Surprisingly Stretchy Bind Off.		
afterthought heel	Pick up heel sts and work the heel of your choice.		
finishing	Once your sock is finished, fold down the cuff at the yo rnd and loosely sew the first rnd to the last rnd on the inside.		

Modifying the pattern

However you manipulate this pattern, you need to make sure that you start (if working top down) or end (if working toe up) the body of your sock with an even number of stitches, in order to accommodate the even number needed for the picot cuff.

If we look at the stitch pattern in the body, columns 1 and 6 remain constant, so we can add stitches to them without altering the flow of the lace surrounding them.

Adding a purl stitch before column 1 could be one option. Another would be to change purl column 6 to a [p1, k1, p1] triplet. Below are two examples that show how you can alter the stitch count of your sock:

# of sts in original sock	# of pattern repeats
60	6
70	7
80	8

Suppose we decided to alter the pattern by working a pfb increase in place of the first p1 in round 7. Then on round 14, we could again change that first p1 to a pfb:

# of sts increased on each increase round	# of sts after Rnd 7	# of sts after Rnd 14
6	66	72
7	77	84
8	88	96

Alternatively, we could change the stitch in column 6 of the chart to a [p1, k1, p1] triplet:

# of sts increased	new # of sts in sock
6 × 2 = 12	72
7 × 2 = 14	84
8 × 2 = 16	96

Notice that in this case the end stitch count is the same, regardless of which path you choose. Which method you select, then, depends entirely on your aesthetic choice.

Gaia

This primal mother goddess of the Greeks symbolizes mother Earth. She is a strong, complete goddess, from whom all others came. The bold stitch pattern on this sock looks equally beautiful as a calf- or knee-high sock.

MATERIALS

Unique Sheep Luxe (75% superwash merino, 25% tussah silk; 400 yds per 100g set), 1 set; sample shown in Pewter

US #1.5/2.5mm needles for working in the round: dpns, 2 short circulars or 1 longer circular

Cable needle
About 4 yds of waste cotton yarn in a similar weight

SIZE & FIT

Average foot circumference: 9 (11.5, 13.5)"
Sample shown in smallest size.

GAUGE

Patt repeat (18 sts × 32 rnds) = 2.25" wide × 3" high

PATTERN NOTES

For tips on working with Gradiance yarns, visit www.theuniquesheep.com/tutorials/gradiancesocks

Top-down version

See page 115 for chart key.

Cuff pattern

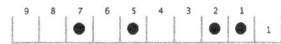

Leg and foot pattern

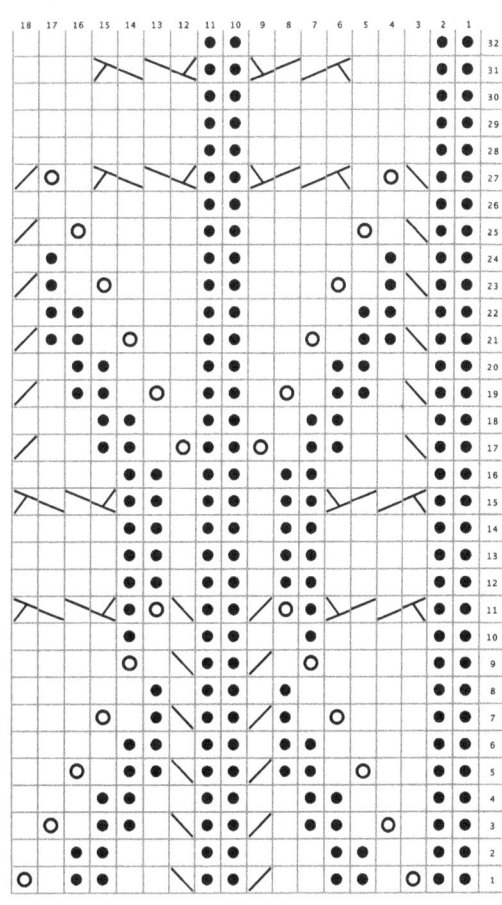

GAIA TOP-DOWN WORKSHEET			
cast-on method	Choose your preferred cast-on method.		
circumference	9"	11.5"	13.5"
# of sts to cast on	72 sts	90 sts	108 sts
# of rnds per inch	10.5 rnds per inch		
length of cuff	3"	3"	3"
# of rnds in cuff	32 rnds	32 rnds	32 rnds
# of sts in leg	72 sts	90 sts	108 sts
leg length	Use your own leg length.		
# of rnds in leg	Work out your own # of rnds by multiplying leg length by 10.5 (number of rnds per inch).		
# of sts for afterthought heel	36 sts	44 sts	54 sts
foot pattern	Work 36 sts in patt for front of sock; knit rem 36 sts with waste yarn, and then re-knit them with project yarn. Continue to work front of sock in patt and sole sts in stockinette.	Work 46 sts in patt for front of sock; knit rem 44 sts with waste yarn, and then re-knit them with project yarn. Continue to work front of sock in patt and sole sts in stockinette.	Work 54 sts in patt for front of sock; knit rem 54 sts with waste yarn, and then re-knit them with project yarn. Continue to work front of sock in patt and sole sts in stockinette.
length of foot minus toe	Use your own foot length.		
# of rnds in foot	Multiply foot length by rnds per inch (10.5).		
toe type			
toe	Divide sts so you have 2 equal groups. If you have an odd number, add an extra decrease to one of the groups as you start your decrease pattern. Follow the toe pattern that best fits your toe in chapter 7.		
closure method	Join rem toe sts using kitchener stitch or 3-needle bind off.		
heel	Pick up heel sts and work the heel of your choice.		

Toe-up version

Cuff pattern

Leg and foot pattern

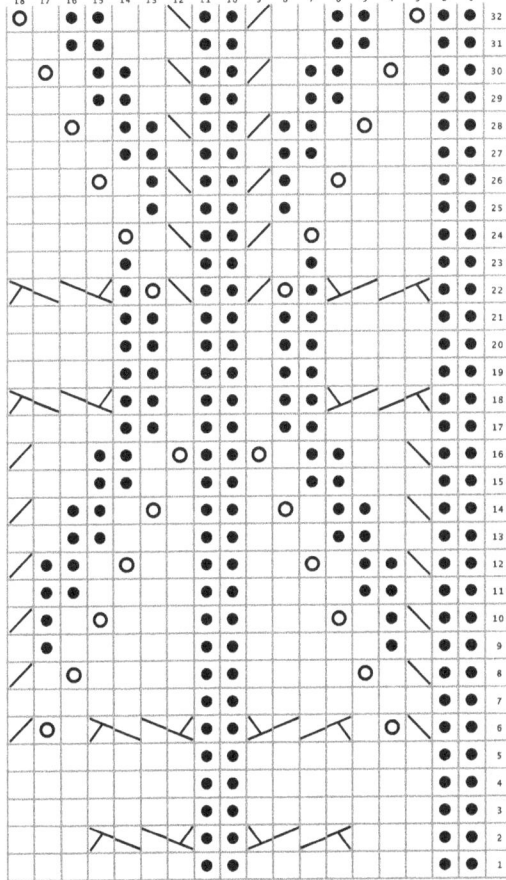

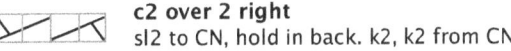

	knit
	knit stitch
•	**purl**
	purl stitch
O	**yo**
	Yarn Over
\	**ssk**
	Slip one stitch as if to knit, Slip another stitch as if to knit. Insert left-hand needle into front of these 2 stitches and knit them together
/	**k2tog**
	Knit two stitches together as one stitch
	c2 over 2 left
	sl 2 to CN, hold in front. k2, k2 from CN
	c2 over 2 right
	sl2 to CN, hold in back. k2, k2 from CN

GAIA TOE-UP WORKSHEET			
cast-on method	Choose your preferred cast-on method.		
circumference	9"	11.5"	13.5"
# of rnds per inch	10.5 rnds per inch		
Toe	Work a toe that ends with 72 sts.	Work a toe that ends with 90 sts.	Work a toe that ends with 108 sts.
foot pattern	Work 36 sts in patt and rem 36 sts in stockinette.	Work 46 sts in patt and rem 44 sts in stockinette.	Work 54 sts in patt and rem 54 sts in stockinette.
foot length	Use your own foot length.		
# of rnds in foot	Work out your own # of rnds by multiplying foot length by 10.5 (number of rnds per inch).		
# of sts for afterthought heel	36 sts	44 sts	54 sts
afterthought heel prep rnd	Work the front of your sock in pattern, and then knit the sole of your foot in waste yarn, and then again with project yarn.		
leg length	Use your own leg length.		
# of rnds in leg	Leg length multiplied by rnd gauge (10.5).		
leg pattern	Work all sts in patt as established.		
cuff length	3"	3"	3"
# of rnds in cuff	32 rnds	32 rnds	32 rnds
bind-off method	Work Jeny's Surprisingly Stretchy Bind Off.		
afterthought heel	Pick up heel sts and work the heel of your choice.		

Gaia

Modifying the pattern

This sock was knitted as a knee-high sock with long increases along columns 1 and 8 until a total of 4 increases had been added across each pattern repeat. A different cuff was designed using the 18 sts:

Row 1 (RS): K2, [p1, k tbl] twice, p1, c2 over 2 right, p1, k2, p1, c2 over 2 left, p1, k tbl, p1.
Row 2 (WS): K1, p tbl, k1, p4, k1, p2, k1, p4, [k1, p tbl] twice, k1, p2.

Row 3: K2, [p1, k tbl] twice, p1, k4, p1, k2, p1, k4, p1, k tbl, p1.
Row 4: K1, p tbl, k1, p4, k1, p2, k1, p4, k1, [p tbl, k1] twice, p2.

Andraste

With origins in the legends of the Celts, Gauls, and Angles—and a name that means, "the invincible one"—Andraste was a goddess of war as well as love. Her fierceness on battlefields of all sorts is reflected in the strength of the patterning in her namesake sock. Small medallions protect your foot and leg, giving strength in all endeavors.

MATERIALS

Lorna's Laces Shepherd Sock (80% wool/20% nylon; 435 yds/398m per 100g skein), 1 skein; sample shown in Ysolda

US #1.5/2.5mm needles for working in the round: dpns, 2 short circulars or 1 longer circular

About 4 yds of waste cotton yarn in a similar weight

SIZE & FIT

Average foot circumference: 9 (10.5, 13)" Sample shown in smallest size.

GAUGE

Pattern repeat (16 sts × 26 rnds) = 1.5" wide × 2" high

PATTERN NOTES

This sock pattern lends itself to a long increase or decrease along column 1.

Both versions: cuff

Cuff Rnd: [P1, k1tbl] around.

Top-down version: leg & foot

See page 121 for chart key.

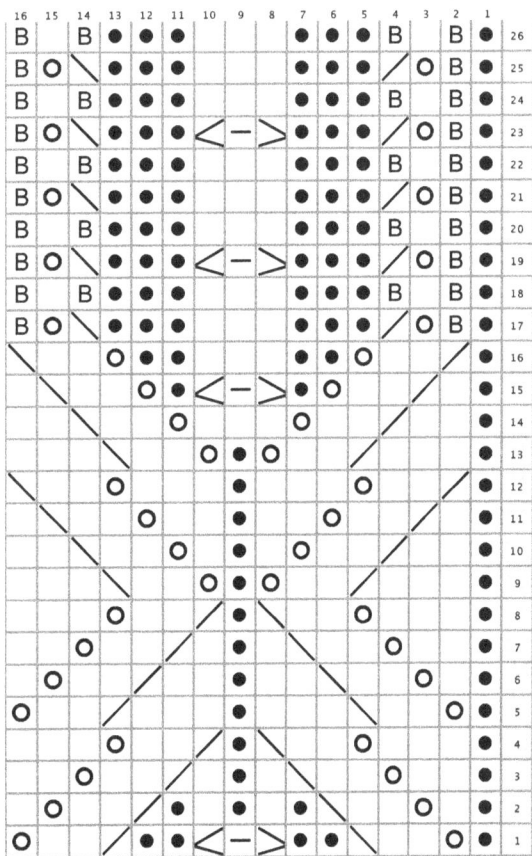

ANDRASTE TOP DOWN WORKSHEET			
cast-on method	Choose your preferred cast-on method.		
circumference	9"	10.5"	13"
# of sts to cast on	80 sts	96 sts	112 sts
# of rnds per inch	13 rnds per inch		
length of cuff	3"	3"	3"
# of rnds in cuff	39 rnds	39 rnds	39 rnds
# of sts in leg	80 sts	96 sts	112 sts
leg length	Use your own leg length.		
# of rnds in leg	Work out your own # of rnds by multiplying leg length by 13 (number of rnds per inch).		
# of sts for afterthought heel	32 sts	48 sts	48 sts
foot pattern	Work 48 sts in patt for front of sock; knit rem 32 sts with waste yarn, and then re-knit them with project yarn. Continue to work front of sock in patt and sole sts in stockinette.	Work 48 sts in patt for front of sock; knit rem 48 sts with waste yarn, and then re-knit them with project yarn. Continue to work front of sock in patt and sole sts in stockinette.	Work 64 sts in patt for front of sock; knit rem 48 sts with waste yarn, and then re-knit them with project yarn. Continue to work front of sock in patt and sole sts in stockinette.
length of foot minus toe	Use your own foot length.		
# of rnds in foot	Multiply foot length by rnds per inch (13).		
toe type			
toe	Divide sts so you have 2 equal groups. If you have an odd number, add an extra decrease to one of the groups as you start your decrease pattern. Follow the toe pattern that best fits your toe in chapter 7.		
closure method	Join rem toe sts using kitchener stitch or 3-needle bind off.		
heel	Pick up heel sts and work the heel of your choice.		

Toe-up version: leg & foot

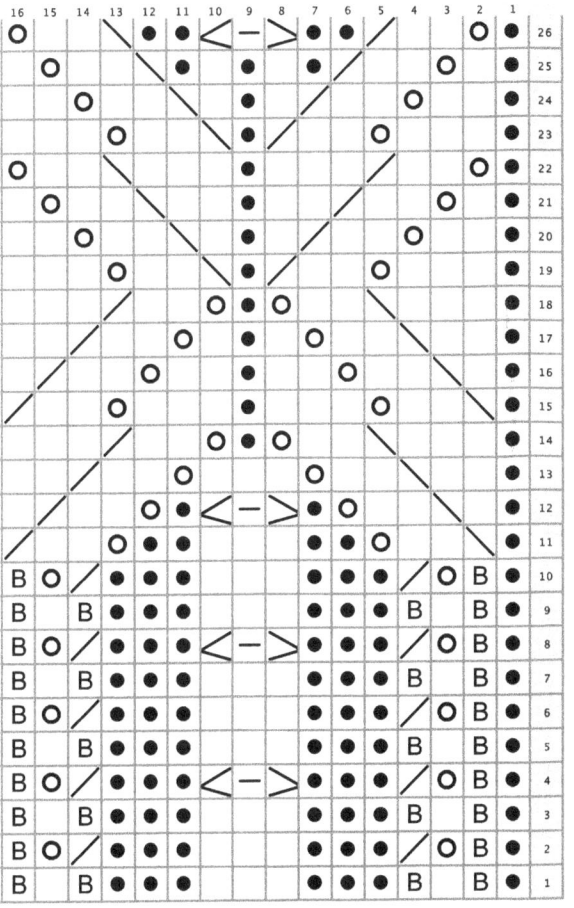

•	**purl** purl stitch
B	**knit tbl** Knit stitch through back loop
☐	**knit** knit stitch
O	**yo** Yarn Over
╱	**k2tog** Knit two stitches together as one stitch
<–>	**3 st wrap** With yarn in back, slip next 3 sts to LH needle, bring yarn to front and slip sts back to RH needle, then knit the 3 sts
╲	**ssk** Slip one stitch as if to knit, Slip another stitch as if to knit. Insert left-hand needle into front of these 2 stitches and knit them together

Big Foot Knits—Andi Smith

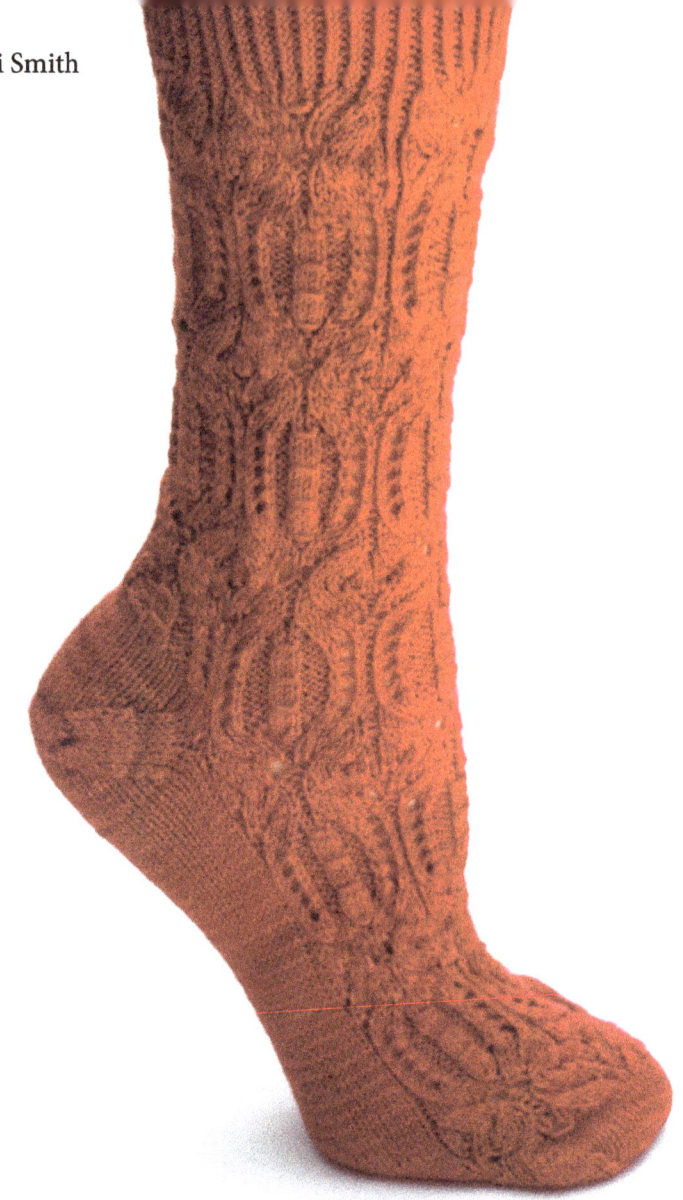

Modifying the pattern

I saved this pattern for last because it poses some challenges when it comes to modification. As you can see, it has a 16-column-wide stitch pattern where only the first column has an unchanging stitch.

While that means that this would not be a good pattern for short increases or decreases, it is well suited for the longer variety, however. Like many of the previous patterns, you could make the increases all purl, or create an additional (p1, k1, p1) triplet. You could even add 3 stitches in the form of the knit/3st-wrap pattern at the beginning of each repeat. So, although it looks like there isn't really much room for change in this stitch pattern, look again—there's more than you think!

ANDRASTE TOE-UP WORKSHEET			
cast-on method	Choose your preferred cast-on method.		
circumference	9"	10.5"	13"
# of rnds per inch	13 rnds per inch		
toe	Work a toe that ends with 80 sts.	Work a toe that ends with 96 sts.	Work a toe that ends with 112 sts.
foot pattern	Work 48 sts in patt (3 reps) and rem 32 sts in stockinette.	Work 48 sts in patt (3 reps) and rem 42 sts in stockinette.	Work 64 sts in patt (4 reps) and rem 48 sts in stockinette.
foot length	Use your own foot length.		
# of rnds in foot	Work out your own # of rnds by multiplying foot length by 13 (number of rnds per inch).		
# of sts for afterthought heel	32 sts	42 sts	48 sts
afterthought heel prep rnd	Work the front of your sock in pattern, and then knit the sole of your foot in waste yarn, and then again with project yarn.		
leg length	Use your own leg length.		
# of rnds in leg	Leg length multiplied by rnd gauge (13).		
leg pattern	Work all sts in patt as established.		
cuff length	3"	3"	3"
# of rnds in cuff	39 rnds	39 rnds	39 rnds
bind-off method	Work Jeny's Surprisingly Stretchy Bind Off.		
afterthought heel	Pick up heel sts and work the heel of your choice.		

APPENDICES

Techniques, abbreviations, and sock care

Cast ons and bind offs are integral parts of your sock knitting experience. One looks forward to working them because they denote the beginning and end of your project. However, they are important for another reason: these beginning and ending techniques form an important part of the structure of your socks. Your cuffs need to be stretchy enough to comfortably ease over your widest body part, but also springy enough to bounce back into place and not affect the gauge of your welt for top-down socks. Your cast ons and bind offs need to fall into that "just right" area: neither so tight that they pucker the fabric, nor so loose that you have holes at the end of your toes.

One of the finest things about knitters, in my mind, is their inventiveness. There are myriad methodologies when it comes to both the cast on and the bind off. Each has its merits. However, I've found that for socks, the following are the best.

Cast ons for top-down socks

A top-down cast on should be able to stretch to more than twice its width and then bounce back to its original state. Whether a particular cast on will succeed at this or not depends partly on the type of yarn you are using. Obviously, something with a high cotton or nylon content will not have the spring of a well-plied merino. However, you can achieve a lot of this bounce-back through your choice of cast on.

By far my favorite in this category is the German Twisted (sometimes also called the Twisted German) cast on. This cast on has everything you could ask for as the foundation of a rib pattern. Somewhat similar to the long-tail cast on, but with an extra twist, it has a depth and springiness that is unparalleled.

No one teaches this technique better than Lucy Neatby, and I won't even attempt to surpass her. If you're unfamiliar with this cast on, follow the link below for a superb tutorial. Practice for a while and get comfortable with the muscle movements before starting your first sock. Work a few rows of rib to see just how sproingy it is!

- www.youtube.com/watch?v=Af1xpkBBYxs

The long-tail method of casting on is similar to the German Twisted, but uses less yarn, has one less twist in its construction and therefore is not as springy or stretchable. A rather fabulous tutorial can be found on Knitty, here:

- www.knitty.com/ISSUEsummer05/FEATsumo5TT.html

Many people find that holding two needles together or using a much larger needle for the cast on helps to create a stretchier fabric. However, I'd caution to do this gingerly as it may affect the gauge of the first few rounds of your cuff. Experiment and see what works best for you!

Bind offs for toe-up socks

As with top-down cast ons, the bind off for a toe-up sock must have a great deal of springiness and stretchability without compromising the gauge and pattern of the welt that it's attached to.

In my mind, there's only one bind off that works extremely well for this purpose, and that is Jeny's Surprisingly Stretchy Bind Off, detailed here:

- knitty.com/ISSUEfall09/FEATjssbo.php

Jeny's clever technique is everything in a bind off that German Twisted is in a cast on.

Cast ons for toe-up socks

When you're choosing a cast on for toe-up socks, consider that immediately after you cast on, you will be knitting in straight stockinette, so the springy cast ons that are so perfect for ribbing are not for you. Instead, you need something that creates a seamless transition between the top and bottom of your sock.

There are two serious contenders when it comes to a toe-up cast on: one that is worked provisionally and then kitchenered, and another one that does the whole thing in one step.

For a provisional cast on, either a crochet or two-color method are your best choice. Each type creates a workable-now/workable-later stitch, and each are equally acceptable.

For a crocheted provisional cast on, check out this tutorial:

- www.knitpicks.com/wptutorials/crocheted-provisional-cast-on/

For two-color and other provisional cast ons, see this Knitting Daily video:

- www.youtube.com/watch?v=GSwG6SJ1z2I

My personal favorite and go-to cast on method for toe-up socks has to be Judy's Magic Cast On:

- knitty.com/ISSUEspring06/FEATmagiccaston.html

This cast on creates a truly seamless fabric that doesn't need the further manipulation that the provisional cast ons do. I love the fluidity of hand movements that you use as you create the stitches in this one; it's lovely to do, and the results cannot be beaten.

Bind offs for top-down socks

Again, you have two choices when it comes to binding off the toe stitches for your top-down sock: the three-needle bind off or the kitchener stitch. Both are great. Newer knitters tend to work the three-needle bind off as it is ostensibly the same as regular knitting. However, it leaves a seam in your socks. The more adventurous knitter usually ends up with kitchener stitch, which grafts the two sides of your sock together seamlessly.

For both techniques, I can recommend Stitch Diva Studios' very informative tutorials, which have clear pictures and good, concrete steps to follow:

- www.stitchdiva.com/tutorials/knitting/kitchener-stitch

- www.stitchdiva.com/tutorials/knitting/three-needle-bind-off

Whichever method you choose, remember to practice to ensure that your gauge remains constant even in these last stitches.

Blocking and caring for your socks

There are differing opinions when it comes to blocking, especially where socks are concerned—after all, they're going to stretch out on your feet, right?

While this is certainly the case, it could (and should) also be argued that blocking is a worthwhile endeavor. When a knitted item—especially one with a stitch pattern that is more complex than stockinette—is wetted, the stitch pattern seems to be more crisp, each stitch more defined, and the "hand" of the created fabric is much more pleasing. It's as if the whole sock breathes a sigh of relief and relaxes.

I recommend using a wool wash, such as Soak or Eucalan, every time you wash your socks, but especially that first time. Not only will you be blocking your socks, but also washing away any residue that may be left from the dyeing or manufacturing—not to mention knitting—process. Follow the directions on your specific wool wash, but as a rule of thumb, be sure to:

- Use tepid water.

- Fully submerge your socks and give them a squeeze underwater a couple of times to make sure all the fibers are saturated. To further ensure saturation, let your socks soak for at least 15 minutes.

- Just like conventional laundering, be sure not to mix your colors, especially the first few times you wash new socks. Sometimes the residual dye can play havoc with other items.

- Gently squeeze out water from your socks, then roll them in a towel to get as much water out as possible.

- Lay the socks on a towel to dry. I like to pop mine on top of the tumble dryer, or outside in a shady spot.

And that's all there is to blocking and caring for your socks. Take good care of your socks and they will take good care of you.

Acknowledgments

It's a bit daft that my name is on the cover of this book, when so very many people were involved in making it happen. I wish your names could be on there, too!

Kate Atherley, tech editor extraordinaire, gets the biggest bundle of thanks. You took my rough thoughts, my sketchy maths, and my outlandish ideas and turned them into cohesive concepts, all with grace and humor and without laughing at me! Thanks, Kate.

The team at CP are all incredible. Shannon Okey, your patience, understanding and encouragement are invaluable gifts—thank you for sharing them with me. My thanks to my phenomenal editor, Elizabeth Green Musselman. You are truly inspiring—I want to be you when I grow up! Heather Ordover gets huge thanks for being my personal cheering squad. Thank you for believing in me, and kicking me in the bum when I needed it!

Major thanks go out to my sample knitters for their talents and patience. Mary Bethel, Stacy Perry, Marla Gardner, Amber Peirce, Melanie Clark, Jamie Henderson, Melissa Thompson, Chris Vanderslice, Summer Ouderkirk, Katrina E Gile, Olga Vakhrameeva, Zona Sherman, Susan Flek, Jessamyn Leib, Jen Kelley, and Nicole Kent. Do you see the beautiful socks you created? Thank you!

Eternal thanks to MJ Kim for her beautiful illustrations.

Monster thanks to Jillian Moreno for saying nice things about me, and to Amy Singer and Jen Hansen for the encouragement and for letting me share their superior knowledge.

Beautiful socks wouldn't be what they are without beautiful yarn. I was lucky enough to have the very best yarn companies—many, many thanks to each of you!

Knit Picks	Madelinetosh	String Theory Colorworks
Cephalopod Yarns	Three Irish Girls	Spud & Chloë
Shibui	The Unique Sheep	Lorna's Laces
Malabrigo	Yarn Love	

Many, *many* thanks to the John Fluevog store in Chicago for lending us their amazing shoes for this shoot. It was very difficult not to keep them all! The wood-soled Fluevogs shown with the Gaia pattern are actually Shannon's, from 1993. Still kicking after all these years. Find out more at fluevog.com

Finally, I'd like to thank all my friends for their support, encouragement, laughter and utter awesomeness. Miriam, Amanda, Amy, Julie, my Akron SnB girls, Heather, Stephannie, Anna, Traci, Kristi, and Sarah. You continue to inspire me.

About the author

Andi Smith lives in Ohio with her husband, two sons, a dog, and cats—and is a new mom to 16 adorable chickens. Andi has been knitting and crocheting for over 40 years, and enjoys it as much now as when she was a small child. Andi is lucky enough to work as a tech editor in the knitting industry, as well as a designer and blogger. She volunteers as a special education advocate, and uses knitting as therapy.

About Cooperative Press

More books to expand your knitting skill set

Bargello Knits by Patty Nance

Knit Accessories by Kate Atherley

Beyond Knit & Purl by Kate Atherley

...and we have many more sock books coming soon!

Cooperative Press (formerly anezka media) was founded in 2007 by Shannon Okey, a voracious reader as well as writer and editor, who had been doing freelance acquisitions work, introducing authors with projects she believed in to editors at various publishers.

Although working with traditional publishers can be very rewarding, there are some books that fly under their radar. They're too avant-garde, or the marketing department doesn't know how to sell them, or they don't think they'll sell 50,000 copies in a year.

5,000 or 50,000. Does the book matter to that 5,000? Then it should be published.

In 2009, Cooperative Press changed its named to reflect the relationships we have developed with authors working on books. We work together to put out the best quality books we can and share in the proceeds accordingly.

Thank you for supporting independent publishers and authors.

Join our mailing list for information on upcoming books!

WWW.COOPERATIVEPRESS.COM

www.ingramcontent.com/pod-product-compliance
Lightning Source LLC
Chambersburg PA
CBHW080923170426
43201CB00016B/2246